"...In nineteen years of teaching language arts, this is the finest vocabulary program I have ever seen. My students like them so much I use them as a reward when other studies have been completed. I definitely recommend them to parents and educators alike..."

Nancy Wiseman
Language Arts Specialist
Mariner High School

"...The great thing about Vocabutoons is they are applicable for everyone, from junior high students to college professors, everyone!..."

Jack Redding
Former School Superintendent
Palm Beach County

"...Vocabutoons worked wonders with my students. Those who benefited the most were those who normally have the most difficulty with vocabulary entries..."

Melissa Skinner
English teacher
Cape Coral High

"...A splendid new tool for S.A.T. prep and students in special education programs!..."

Larry Marsh
Language Arts Educator
North Ft. Myers High

"...So entertaining, it teaches itself...it is a joy for a teacher to have her entire class alert and joining in together as they learn....Vocabutoons is a unique learning process students respond well to, resulting in greater learning and retention..."

Sharon Kramer
Mariner High

VOCABULARY CARTOONS

Building an Educated Vocabulary with Visual Mnemonics

Sam, Max, and Bryan Burchers

New Monic Books, Inc.

Manufactured in the United States of America.
Library of Congress Catalog Card Number: 96-96399
ISBN: 0-9652422-8-5
Illustrations: Joseph Toth, Lee Horton, David Horton, Luke Wilson,
& John Telford
Cover Design: Bryan Burchers, D.T. Publishing
Setup & Typography: Sam Burchers III

Library of Congress Cataloging-in-Publication Data
Burchers, Sam
    Vocabulary Cartoons
    Sam Burchers, Jr., Sam Burchers, III & Bryan Burchers
            p.   cm.
    Includes index.
    ISBN 0-9652422-8-5
    1. Vocabulary Cartoons-United States.
II. Title

                                                    96-96399

New Monic Books
314-C Tamiami Trail
Punta Gorda, FL 33950
(941) 575-6669 $12.95

Acknowledgments

The Educators

Our gratitude to the following educators in Southwest Florida who had the foresight and initiative to introduce mnemonic cartoon test programs in their schools and classrooms. It was through their efforts that vocabulary cartoons have been proven to be a dynamic new technique in building a more educated vocabulary:

North Fort Myers High School
Ed Stickles, Princ.
Larry Marsh

Cape Coral High School
Karyl Davis, Asst. Princ. Cur.
Melisa Skinner

Murdock Middle School
Lou Long, Princ.
Debbie Moore
William Valella

Alva Middle School
Jerry Demming, Asst. Princ. Cur.
Jean Riner

Port Charlotte Middle School
Clyde Hoff, Princ.
Dianne Woolley

Mariner High School
Bonnie Hill, Asst. Princ. Cur.
Judy Baxley
Jennifer Basler
Sharon Kramer
Nancy Wiseman

The Artists

Our special thanks to staff artists Joe Toth, Gene Ostmark, Bryan Burchers, Lee Horton and Dave Horton, and contributing artists Luke Wilson and John Telford. Their collective talents provided the essential quality of zany humor and outrageous bizarreness that make cartoon mnemonics memorable.

Contents

Introduction

What This Book Is All About

Welcome to the world of humorous cartoons that introduce proven mnemonic memory techniques into the vocabulary learning experience.

A mnemonic is a device that helps you remember something by associating what you are trying to remember with something you already know. Memory experts agree that mnemonics are the surest, fastest and easiest way to remember names, places, events, words and anything else you want to remember.

If you are like most people, you want to learn words as efficiently and as rapidly as possible. With Vocabulary Cartoons it is possible to learn hundreds of new words over a single weekend - it's that easy!

In any public library there are numerous books on memory techniques. Without exception, experts speak of the science of mnemonics as one of the most important and basic tools of memory.

For example, U.S. Marines are taught a mnemonic based on the letters P.P.P.F.P., which means "Prior Planning Prevents Faulty Performance."

Rhymes and poems also serve as mnemonics. Perhaps the most common childhood mnemonic for remembering a historical date is that old limerick, "Columbus sailed the ocean blue in fourteen hundred and ninety two."

Remember that one? Once you have learned it, how could you ever forget it?

In addition to auditory mnemonics, there are visual mnemonics, where you create in your mind's eye a mental image of whatever it is you wish to remember.

When my son, Bryan, was in grade school, he had trouble remembering the definition of the word ALOOF.

"What does ALOOF rhyme with?"

"ROOF," he replied.

"What's on the ROOF?" I asked.

"Our cat, Snowball," he said.

I suggested Bryan make a mental picture with both words in it. We came up with this one: "Snowball was so ALOOF, when guests came she hid on the ROOF."

Thereafter, whenever Bryan heard the word ALOOF, he would think of ROOF, then in turn visualize his cat, Snowball, hiding on the ROOF because Snowball was ALOOF.

This procedure is what the experts in memory mnemonics, such as Harry Lorayne in his book, *The Page-a-Minute Book*, recommend. Take a word you wish to learn, link it to a word, or a group of words, you already know. Now visualize a mental picture of a scene in which both words play an integral part. Make the mental picture as bizarre and ridiculous as you like. Bizarre events have an impact that stimulates the memory. Commonplace events do not.

Most teachers have favorite mnemonics they pass along to their students. However, the occasional mnemonics introduced in classrooms have been used randomly and are rarely part of the formal curriculum.

Now for the first time ever, we are introducing an entire book of mnemonics.

Practically all memory books ask the reader to create his or her own visual mnemonic images. With many simple words, such as our example, "aloof," it is reasonably easy to do. However, in the case of abstract words, mnemonic images can be very difficult to create.

For example, try to visualize mental pictures for the words "triumvirate" and "peregrination." Anything come to mind? Probably not.

Therein lies the fallacy of visual mnemonics you are asked to conjure up yourself. The time element is devastating. You could spend hours creating appropriate visualizations for only a dozen words. The net result is most students give up on the entire mnemonics process.

Not so with Vocabulary Cartoons, where we provide word associations and visual images that make study easy and entertaining. You will be amazed at the magic of these specialized cartoons as your vocabulary grows and grows almost effortlessly.

Years from now, whenever you hear a word from this book, odds are the cartoon of that word will appear in your mind's eye in a flash. That is how indelible and unforgettable good mnemonics can be.

Who Would Most Benefit From This Book?

Vocabulary Cartoons are designed for anyone wishing to build a stronger vocabulary. However, they are particularly recommended for students studying for Pre-Scholastic Aptitude Tests (P.S.A.T.), Scholastic Aptitude Tests (S.A.T.) and Graduate Record Exams (G.R.E.); older students in Adult Education courses, English as a Second Language (E.S.O.L.) students; those in Exceptional Student Education (E.S.E.) programs and Attention Deficit Disorder (A.D.D.) programs.

How To Use This Book

Each page consists of five elements:

1. The **main word**. The word you wish to learn. It is followed by the phonetic pronunciation and a definition.
Example: MUSTER (MUS tur), to collect or gather; an act of inspection or critical examination.

2. The **link word**. The link word is a simple word or words which rhyme or sound like the main word.
Example: MUSTARD

3. The **caption**. The caption connects the main word and the linking word in a sentence.
Example: Each morning the MUSTARD troops are MUSTERED for roll call.

4. The **cartoon**. The caption is made into a bizarre or humorous cartoon which incorporates the main word and the linking word into a visual mnemonic.
Example:

"Each morning the MUSTARD troops are
MUSTERED for roll call."

5. **Sample sentences** in different context.

Example: In 1836, the Texans at the Alamo MUSTERED all the troops available to defend against the invading Mexican Army.

Once you make the word association connection, whenever you hear the word "MUSTER," the linking word MUSTARD will come to mind along with the visual image of the MUSTARD troops MUSTERED for roll call.

You may think of another link word that works better for you than the one provided in this book. That is okay, go ahead and do so. The main goal is to introduce you to the power of mnemonics and how well it can work for you.

Use the book like flash cards, flipping through the cartoons one by one from front to back. After a time you will find that the main word and its associating link word belong together and the visual image of the cartoon automatically appears in your mind's eye. When this happens, the definition of the main word becomes fixed in your mind.

There is an old Chinese proverb which says, "What you see once is worth what you hear a hundred times." This is another way of saying "a picture is worth a thousand words."

The words selected in this book are those frequently found in the S.A.T. and G.R.E. How well you do on the verbal skill sections of either test is almost exclusively determined by your vocabulary skills.

Remember that approximately 90% of university courses require reading comprehension. And to be a good reader you must have an extensive vocabulary.

School Test Results

The effectiveness of vocabulary mnemonics as a faster, easier learning tool has been established in six independent school tests in Southwest Florida. These tests took place in 1995 and 1996 and involved hundreds of students at different grade levels.

In Port Charlotte Middle School, Mrs. Woolley's eighth grade class scored 180% higher test grades with this book than did the control class that had rote memory study books.

At Cape Coral High School, English teacher Melissa Skinner's tenth grade class scored 105% higher, and had six times more "A's" than did the control tenth grade class without theVocabulary Cartoon books.

In Larry Marsh's ninth grade English classes at North Fort Myers High, mnemonics helped E.S.E. students achieve test results that equaled those of non-E.S.E. students.

Altogether, students with Vocabulary Cartoons scored an average 72% higher marks than did the control students that used rote memory study books.

Vocabulary Cartoons are not intended to replace traditional vocabulary study books. However, they are a valuable building block adjunct to the overall vocabulary learning process.

CHATTEL

(chatel)
an item of personal, movable
property; slave
Link: CATTLE

"Tex's CATTLE were his CHATTEL."

❑ The bank held a CHATTEL mortgage on all our office equipment, chairs, computers and even our electric clock.

❑ Please do not order me around Lady Boswell, I am neither your servant nor your CHATTEL.

❑ The CHATTEL belonging to Herodotos of Athens at his death were sixteen slaves, seven horses, six hunting dogs and three midget gladiators.

AUSTERE
(aw STEER)
stern, as in manner; without excess,
unadorned, severely simple and plain
Link: STEER

*"An AUSTERE STEER is no
fun at a party."*

- ❑ Jill's father was AUSTERE, rarely smiled and was always stern with her about having dates with boys he didn't know.

- ❑ The AUSTERITY of life in the village was understandable. Many were jobless and evidence of poverty was everywhere.

- ❑ Her home was AUSTERELY decorated, very plain furniture without frills and only items that were necessary.

LAMENT
(la MINT)
to express sorrow or regret;
to mourn
Link: CEMENT

*"We LAMENT that Joe got
buried in CEMENT."*

- ❏ The song, "Cowboy's LAMENT," is a ballad about the lonely life of those who drive cattle for a living.

- ❏ The nation LAMENTS the passing of the President while at the same time celebrating his achievements while in office.

- ❏ It is LAMENTABLE that Roscoe quit college in his sophomore year; his professors considered him the brightest engineering student in his class.

17

ALOOF
(uh LOOF)
distant, reserved in manner;
uninvolved
Link: **ROOF**

*"Snowball, the cat, was so ALOOF when
guests came she hid on the ROOF."*

- ❏ Most everyone thought Theodore ALOOF when actually he was only very shy.

- ❏ Nothing ruins a fine dinner at a good restaurant like an ALOOF waiter who makes the entire experience uncomfortable.

- ❏ At the wedding reception, the bride's relatives were very ALOOF, hardly speaking to the groom's guests and family.

CEREBRAL
(suh REE brul)
of or relating to the brain;
an intellectual person
Link: **CEREAL**

*"Eat your CEREAL so you'll grow up and be
CEREBRAL like your father."*

☐ CEREBRAL for a football player, the wily Kansas
quarterback rarely called a play that wasn't well
planned and thought out.

☐ Dr. Clark was too CEREBRAL to be a boy scout
leader. Instead of saying "pitch your tents over by
the cliff," he would confuse everyone with his big
words and say, "construct the canvas shelters in
the proximity of the promontory."

INCONGRUOUS
(in KAHN grew us)
not appropriate, unsuited to the
surroundings; not fitting in
Link: **IN CONGRESS**

*"The new Alaskan senator's presence IN CONGRESS
was INCONGRUOUS."*

❑ Ed appeared INCONGRUOUS wearing his tuxedo
on an old-fashioned hayride.

❑ The INCONGRUITY with Joseph's chosen career
was that he had a Ph.D. in chemistry, but preferred
to work as a mullet fisherman.

❑ INCONGRUOUSLY, Dianne spent several days a
week at the library, even though she professed that
she didn't like to read.

BULWARK

(BULL wurk)
a defensive wall; something serving
as a principle defense

Link: **BULL WORK**

"BULLS WORK building a BULWARK."

- ❏ Quebec City is the only city in North America with a BULWARK built entirely around it.

- ❏ The budget for national defense is an economic burden for all taxpayers, but we must never forget our armed services are the BULWARK of defense for the nation.

- ❏ Our mother was a BULWARK against bad times; no matter how bad things became she always wore a smile and had a cheerful word.

CONNOISSEUR
(kahn uh SUR)
an expert, particularly in
matters of art and taste

Link: **KING OF SEWER**

*"The KING OF the SEWER is a
CONNOISSEUR of garbage."*

❑ My uncle is a CONNOISSEUR of fine wines.

❑ Art dealer, Jorge Guizar, is a CONNOISSEUR of
Mexican art of the 19th century.

❑ When it came to coins, Jerry proclaimed he was a
CONNOISSEUR, because he had collected them
all his life.

CACOPHONY
(kuh KAFH uh nee)
harsh sounds
Link: COUGH

"A CACOPHONY of COUGHING."

❏ A CACOPHONY isn't noise alone, it is disturbing noise such as when people shout all at once.

❏ Gene thinks all rock music is a CACOPHONY to be avoided whenever possible.

❏ An unpleasant CACOPHONY of sound was produced as the orchestra tuned their instruments. But once they began to play together the sounds became euphonious.

EXPUNGE
(ex PUNGE)
to remove; to delete; to erase
Link: **SPONGE**

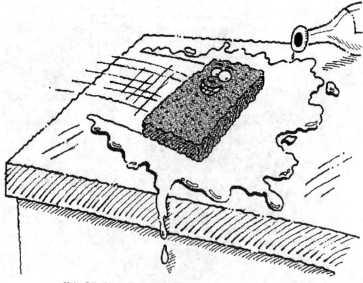

"A SPONGE EXPUNGING a spill."

☐ The judge ordered the clerk to EXPUNGE the lawyer's statement from the record.

☐ The wet and muddy footprints were EXPUNGED with soap and water.

☐ The teacher told Justin EXPUNGING the low grades from his record was not something she was willing to do.

REVIEW #1: Match the word with its definition.

1. chattel - (cattle)
2. austere - (steer)
3. lament - (cement)
4. aloof - (roof)
5. cerebral - (cereal)
6. incongruous - (in congress)
7. bulwark - (bull work)
8. connoisseur - (sewer)
9. cacophony – (cough)
10. expunge – (sponge)

a. reserved in manner
b. harsh sounds
c. personal property
d. unadorned, stern
e. to remove
f. relating to the brain
g. express sorrow
h. an expert in taste
i. not appropriate
j. a principal defense

Fill in the blanks with the appropriate word. The word form may need changing.

1. Most everyone thought Theodore _____ when actually he was only very shy.

2. Quebec City is the only city in North America with a _____ built entirely around it.

3. Gene thinks all rock music is nothing more than a _____ to be avoided whenever possible.

4. Please do not order me around, Lady Boswell, I am neither your servant nor your _____.

5. Phil appeared _____ wearing his tuxedo on an old-fashioned hayride.

6. Eat your cereal so you'll grow up and be _____ like your father.

7. The judge ordered the clerk to _____ the lawyer's statement from the record.

8. Jill's father was _____, rarely smiled and was always stern with her.

9. The nation _____ the passing of the president while at the same time celebrating his achievements.

10. An art dealer all his life, Juan Hernandez was a _____ of Mexican art of the 19th century.

25

TRENCHANT
(TREN chunt)
cutting, incisive, having a sharp
point; caustic, sarcastic
Link: **TRENCH ANT**

*"A TRENCHANT mouth is characteristic of the
famous Madagascar TRENCH ANT."*

❑ Roger's TRENCHANT remarks at the budget
meeting could be explained by the fact that he
knew precisely where the financial problems lay.

❑ The music teacher made numerous TRENCHANT
comments about the band's performance; clearly
she thought the band stunk.

❑ Julia had a TRENCHANT tongue and was always
putting her friends down behind their backs.

PROCRASTINATE
(PRO cras tuh nate)
to put off until a later time
Link: **GRASS HATE**

*"Larry HATED to cut the GRASS and would
PROCRASTINATE about it for weeks."*

❏ Never do today what you can PROCRASTINATE
until tomorrow, a famous husband once said.

❏ Tom would PROCRASTINATE until the last minute
to do his homework.

❏ Wilcox had a PROCRASTINATING personality;
whatever he started, you felt he was probably not
going to finish.

ROSTER
(raw ster)
a list of names; especially of
personnel available for duty
Link: **ROOSTER**

"A ROOSTER on the ROSTER."

- ❑ The football program has a ROSTER for both teams.

- ❑ Tom saw his name on the duty ROSTER.

- ❑ The military is full of all types of ROSTERS; there is a duty ROSTER, a leave ROSTER and even a ROSTER for standing guard.

IMPEDE
(im PEED)
to obstruct or interfere with;
to delay
Link: **SPEED**

*"The job of highway patrolmen is to
IMPEDE SPEEDING motorists."*

❑ He was only my uncle, but he always told me no
matter what, not to let anyone IMPEDE my
ambition to go to medical school.

❑ (Something that IMPEDES is an IMPEDIMENT.)
As a hopeful runner on the school track team,
James Carver's biggest IMPEDIMENT to his foot
speed was his short legs.

FORBEAR
(for BAYR)
to refrain from; to abstain;
to be patient or tolerant
Link: **FOUR BEARS**

"Please FORBEAR feeding the FOUR BEARS."

- ❑ To FORBEAR your opinion on any controversial matter until you have first heard all the facts is generally the wisest course of action.

- ❑ Jonathan said his motto was to never FORBEAR a good party for another time when you can have one today.

- ❑ Henry FORBORE his decision to close the store, deciding to wait until after the Christmas season.

MIGRATORY

(MIE gra tory)
roving, wandering, nomadic
Link: **MY STORY**

"MY STORY is one of many MIGRATORY movements."

❑ Wild geese MIGRATE to Canada in the summers and Mexico in the winters.

❑ Most American Indian tribes in the old west were MIGRATORY and followed the movements of the buffalo.

❑ Fruit pickers are MIGRATORY workers who move from place to place at harvesting time.

EVADE
(ee VADE)
to elude or avoid by cunning; to flee from a pursuer

Link: **BLADE**

"A magician's secret for EVADING BLADES."

- ❑ The escaped prisoners EVADED the authorities by breaking into a church and disguising themselves as nuns.

- ❑ Jane always managed to EVADE helping her sister wash the dinner dishes by claiming she had homework to do.

- ❑ Their romance never really blossomed as their friends expected, because Sarah was the pursuer, but Bill was the EVADER.

EFFACE
(uh FACE)
to rub away
Link: **ERASE**

"How to EFFACE a face by ERASING it."

❑ We came upon a cemetery by the sea. Many of the headstone inscriptions had been EFFACED by the ravages of time, but we could make out many that were well over two hundred years old.

❑ To assure that he left no clues, the thief EFFACED his fingerprints from the stolen car.

❑ Someone vandalized the museum paintings by EFFACING each one with red spray paint.

ASUNDER
(uh SUN dur)
in separate parts; apart from each
other in position
Link: THUNDER

*"The THUNDER tore the young
lovers ASUNDER."*

❑ When the earthquake stopped, and we came up
from our shelter, we found the city had been torn
ASUNDER and not one single building was left
standing.

❑ Our team lost its unity and became a group of
individuals who played entirely for themselves,
ASUNDER from each other.

INCITE
(en SIGHT)
to arouse to action
Link: **FIGHT**

*"The pitcher's bean ball INCITED
the batter to FIGHT."*

❑ The mob was INCITED to riot when the police arrived and began hitting people with their nightsticks.

❑ When Rodney decided that his case was hopeless, nothing the doctors could say would INCITE him to fight his illness.

❑ Waving a stick at Jerry's dog only INCITES him and increases the chance he will bite you.

REVIEW #2: Match the word with its definition.

1. trenchant - (trench ant)
2. procrastinate - (grass hate)
3. roster - (rooster)
4. impede - (speed)
5. forbear - (four bears)
6. migratory – (my story)
7. evade - (blade)
8. efface - (face)
9. asunder - (thunder)
10. incite - (fight)

a. interfere with
b. cutting, sharp
c. list of names
d. arouse to action
e. separate into parts
f. to refrain from
g. to rub away
h. to put off
i. wandering, move
j. elude or avoid

Fill in the blanks with the appropriate word. The word form may need changing.

1. Wild geese _____ to Canada in the summers and Mexico in the winters.

2. The thunder tore the young lovers _____.

3. When the navy ship docked in Hong Kong Harbor, Jeremy was disappointed when he saw the duty _____ had his name on it.

4. Please _____ feeding the four bears.

5. Roger's angry remarks at the meeting were _____, because he knew where the financial problems lay.

6. Larry hated to cut the grass and would _____ about it for weeks.

7. The paintings were vandalized by someone who _____ each one with red spray paint.

8. The job of highway patrolmen is to _____ speeding motorists.

9. The escaped prisoners _____ the authorities by disguising themselves as nuns.

10. The mob was _____ to riot when the police arrived and began clubbing people.

36

QUIXOTIC
(kwik SAHT ik)
idealistic and totally impractical
Link: **IDIOTIC**

"Jim, the messenger, is not IDIOTIC,
he's just QUIXOTIC."

☐ Professor Callan said it is QUIXOTIC of society to ignore the world's environmental problems.

☐ Putting all taxpayers on the honor system is a QUIXOTIC suggestion.

☐ Sue had the most QUIXOTIC ideas of what her life would be like if she ever won the lottery.

BELEAGUER
(be LEE gur)
to besiege; beset, surround, harass
Link: **BIG LEAGUER**

*"The little leaguers BELEAGUERED
the BIG LEAGUERS."*

- ❑ In World War II, the Russian city of Stalingrad was BELEAGUERED by the German Army for five months before it fell to the Germans.

- ❑ During his last year in office, Richard Nixon was a BELEAGUERED president, struggling to fight off the Watergate scandal.

- ❑ In the midst of important negotiations, the union official asked his staff not to BELEAGUER him with insignificant details.

MILIEU
(mill you)
environment or surroundings
Link: **MILDEW**

*"The boys' locker room showers were
a MILIEU of MILDEW."*

☐ After a long sea journey, a sailor on land for the first few days feels out of his MILIEU.

☐ The proper MILIEU for raising a family is a home setting with loving parents who understand child rearing; something every parent must work at and not take for granted.

☐ The New York Stock Exchange is a MILIEU of frenzied activity during trading hours.

HISTRIONIC
(his tree AHN ik)
overly dramatic, theatrical
Link: **HISTORY**

*"Professor Bradley liked his HISTORY on
the HISTRIONIC side."*

❑ As soon as you would mention the word wrinkle,
the middle-aged actress would fall into a state of
HISTRIONIC tears.

❑ Everything Michael said was on the swaggering,
HISTRIONIC side, as if he were the coolest guy
on campus.

❑ The children's HISTRIONICS when they couldn't
find their toys made everyone uncomfortable.

BLUDGEON

(BLUD jun)
a short heavy, thick club that has
one end larger than the other

<u>Link:</u> **DUNGEON**

*"Why do you suppose they have all these
BLUDGEONS in this DUNGEON?"*

❑ There was nothing temperate about the lawyer's
summary to the jury; he BLUDGEONED them
with all the gruesome details of the murder.

❑ Henry's BLUDGEONING accusations about his
neighbor's dog were more than criticisms; he was
trying to intimidate the dog owner into getting rid
of the animal.

❑ The police arrested the lumberjack on suspicion of
BLUDGEONING a co-worker with an axe handle.

41

ARDUOUS
(AHR joo us)
hard, difficult, tiresome
Link: **HARD ON US**

"The ARDUOUS snow-covered trail
is HARD ON US."

- ❑ The assignment given the recruits was ARDUOUS, twenty miles with full packs in the hot sun.

- ❑ Swimming three miles was the most ARDUOUS exercise Jeannie ever had.

- ❑ The long, ARDUOUS boat trip was made even worse by stormy seas and much seasickness.

REMINISCE
(rem uh NISS)
the act or practice of
recalling the past
Link: **RIM MISS**

"Jim never got over his RIM MISS and tortured himself for years REMINISCING about it."

❑ Sometimes when we are feeling nostalgic, my wife and I lie back and listen to the music of the 1960s and REMINISCE about when we were dating and the things we used to do.

❑ The REMINISCENT qualities in his art brought back fond memories of Paris in the 19th century.

OPPORTUNE
(AHP ur tune)
occurring or coming at a
good time
Link: **OPERA TUNE**

"Not an OPPORTUNE time for an OPERA TUNE."

- ❏ An OPPORTUNIST at heart, Ed OPPORTUNELY dropped by Janet's house just as dinner was being served.

- ❏ During the family reunion, Christopher felt it the OPPORTUNE moment for announcing his job promotion.

- ❏ Mrs. Childs, our teacher, said the weekend before our final exam was an OPPORTUNE time for last minute studying.

DULCET
(DULL set)
melodious, soft, soothing
Link: **DULL SIT**

"If you don't like opera, even the most DULCET tones of the finest sopranos make for a DULL SIT."

❑ Senator Kramer was a political campaigner who could hypnotize an audience with sweet words and DULCET tones.

❑ Jeff's parents declared there was nothing DULCET about the rock-and-roll music that shook the house from his room every morning as he dressed for school.

PORCINE

(PORE sein)

reminiscent of or pertaining
to a pig; resembling a pig

Link: **POOR SCENE**

*"It was a POOR SCENE when Mark
arrived with his PORCINE date."*

❑ After an around the world cruise, where each meal
   is a grand feast, Bob and Helen returned home
   with PORCINE figures.

❑ She had a PORCINE attitude about food; that is
   to say she would eat anything and everything.

REVIEW #3: Match the word with its definition.

1. quixotic – (idiotic)
2. beleaguer - (big leaguer)
3. milieu - (mildew)
4. histrionic - (history)
5. bludgeon - (dungeon)
6. arduous - (hard on us)
7. reminisce - (rim miss)
8. opportune – (opera tune)
9. dulcet - (dull sit)
10. porcine - (poor scene)

a. occurring at a good time
b. hard, tiresome
c. surroundings
d. impractical
e. to surround, harass
f. overly dramatic
g. melodious, soothing
h. recalling the past
i. pertaining to a pig
j. a short, heavy club

Fill in the blanks with the appropriate word. The word form may need changing.

1. Standing in the elevator with Michael Jordan, Bryan felt it the _____ time to ask for his autograph.

2. If you've never heard opera, even the most _____ tones of the finest sopranos make for a dull sit.

3. She had a _____ attitude about food; that is to say she would eat anything and everything.

4. The _____ qualities in his art brought back fond memories of Paris in the 19th century.

5. Why do you suppose they have all these _____ in this dungeon.

6. During World War II, the Russian city of Stalingrad was _____ by the German Army.

7. Professor Callan said it was _____ of society to ignore the world's environmental problems.

8. The _____ boat trip was made even worse by stormy seas and much seasickness.

9. The boys' locker room showers were a _____ of mildew.

10. Professor Bradley liked his history on the _____ side.

47

LASSITUDE
(LAS uh tood)
listlessness; torpor, weariness
Link: **LAZY DUDE**

"A LAZY DUDE with LASSITUDE."

- ❑ After eating three servings of Thanksgiving dinner, George succumbed to a feeling of LASSITUDE and fell asleep on the couch.

- ❑ Having worked for the cannery for twenty years without a raise, Charles became discouraged with his employers and approached his daily work with unenthusiastic LASSITUDE.

COTERIE
(KOH tuh ree)
a circle of close associates or friends
Link: **COAT FOR THREE**

*"The maestro and his COTERIE
in a COAT FOR THREE."*

❑ Today's tennis stars rarely travel alone, but with a COTERIE of managers and coaches.

❑ Rock stars have a COTERIE of fans who follow them around like leeches.

❑ You have to be a member of Daisy's COTERIE, or you don't count at all, in the opinion of Daisy.

BALLISTICS

(buh LISS ticks)
the study of the dynamics or flight
characteristics of projectiles

Link: **LIPSTICK**

"BALLISTIC LIPSTICK."

☐ BALLISTICS is a noun, while BALLISTIC is an adjective which means "of projectiles."

☐ Most naval warships carry BALLISTIC missiles.

☐ Detective Culleton specializes in BALLISTICS and is always called to a crime scene whenever a firearm is involved.

AMBIANCE
(AM bee uns)
mood, feeling; general atmosphere
Link: **AMBULANCE**

*"George did not enjoy the AMBIANCE
in the AMBULANCE."*

❑ The AMBIANCE of the locker room after the team lost the championship was depressing.

❑ For their daughter's birthday party, the Jeffersons' created an AMBIANCE of gaiety, decorating the garden with bright balloons and ribbons.

❑ The AMBIANCE in the Italian restaurant was delightful, there was soft music, candlelight and singing waiters.

GIRTH
(girth)
the distance around something; to encircle; to secure
with a band that encircles the body of an animal
Link: **BIRTH**

*"Before giving BIRTH, ladies are quite
large in GIRTH."*

- ❑ Jonathan placed the saddle on top of the horse and
  fastened the GIRTH.

- ❑ Before crawling into a sewer pipe, it is first wise to
  measure the GIRTH.

- ❑ The GIRTH of the planet Earth is about twenty-
  five thousand miles.

ASKEW
(uh SKEW)
to one side; crooked; awry; a
sidelong look of contempt
Link: CUE

"Curly's pool CUE had become ASKEW."

❑ After the flood receded, the bridge was found to be ASKEW of the road which connected to it.

❑ The tire wouldn't fit on the car because in the accident the axle had been bent ASKEW.

❑ The speaker looked ASKEW at the heckler at every interruption.

CUBISM
(KYOO biz um)
a style of art in which the subject matter is
portrayed by geometric forms, especially cubes
Link: **CUBES**

*"By the look of these CUBES, you are an
artist of the school of CUBISM."*

❑ CUBISM is a style of art that stresses abstract
structure at the expense of other pictorial elements
by fragmenting the form of those objects that are
to be depicted.

❑ Pablo Picasso did not originate the CUBISM style
of painting, but he is credited with popularizing it.

CRANNY
(KRAN ee)
a small opening as in a
wall or rock face
Link: **GRANNY**

"GRANNY found a CRANNY."

☐ The secret message was found stuffed into a small CRANNY in the courtyard wall next to the church.

☐ Rock climbers look for any CRANNY where they can get a secure foothold.

☐ We searched the house from top to bottom and never overlooked a single nook or CRANNY.

ENRAGE

(in RAGE)
to put in a rage;
infuriate, anger

Link: **HEN CAGE**

*"An ENRAGED farmer discovering
a fox in the HEN CAGE."*

❑ What ENRAGES my wife is when I forget to wipe
my feet before coming into the house.

❑ Muriel's boss was ENRAGED when he found out
she had gone on her vacation to the Caribbean and
left a lot of unfinished work on her desk.

PROPULSIVE
(PROH pul siv)
the act or process of propelling;
a propelling force
Link: **PROPELLER**

*"PROPELLERS provide the PROPULSIVE force that
PROPEL many transportation vehicles."*

❑ The first ship PROPELLED by a PROPELLER was
invented by Isambard Brunel in 1844.

❑ The champion hit his opponent, Ray Jackson,
with a terrific right cross that PROPELLED him
right into the second row.

❑ Modern submarines are PROPELLED by nuclear
energy.

REVIEW #4: Match the word with its definition.

1. lassitude - (lazy dude)
2. coterie - (coat for three)
3. ballistics - (lipstick)
4. ambiance - (ambulance)
5. girth - (birth)
6. askew - (cue)
7. cubism - (cube)
8. cranny - (granny)
9. enrage - (hen cage)
10. propulsive - (propeller)

a. to infuriate
b. small opening
c. distance around
d. propelling force
e. the study of projectiles
f. listless, weariness
g. crooked, awry
h. mood, atmosphere
i. style of art
j. close associates

Fill in the blanks with the appropriate word. The word form may need changing.

1. Propellers provide the _____ force that propel many transportation vehicles.

2. The tire wouldn't fit on the car because the axle had been bent _____ in the accident.

3. The _____ of the locker room after the team lost the championship was depressing.

4. What _____ my wife is when I forget to wipe my feet before coming into the house.

5. Today's tennis stars rarely travel alone, but with a _____ of managers and coaches.

6. The secret message was found stuffed into a small _____ in the courtyard wall next to the church.

7. Detective Culleton specializes in _____ and is always called to a crime scene whenever a firearm is involved.

8. The _____ of the planet Earth is about twenty-five thousand miles.

9. After eating three servings of Thanksgiving dinner, George succumbed to a feeling of _____ and fell asleep on the couch.

10. Pablo Picasso did not originate the _____ style of painting, but he is credited with popularizing it.

58

LACONIC
(luh KAHN ik)
brief, using few words
Link: TONIC

*"Grandma was LACONIC when it came time
for Grandpa's TONIC."*

❑ Benjamin's LACONIC speech habits gave him a
reputation for thoughtfulness and intelligence.

❑ The doctor was LACONIC with his patients to
the point of being rude.

❑ The fictional heroes of the old west were usually
cowboys who spoke LACONICALLY, when at all.

HARROWING
(HARE roe ing)
extremely distressed; disturbing
or frightening
Link: **HARE ROWING**

"A HARROWING experience for a HARE ROWING."

❑ After the HARROWING experience when Eddie's main parachute didn't open, and his emergency chute saved him only at the last minute, he vowed never to jump again.

❑ (HARRIED is to be troubled or bothered while HARROWING is to be frightened to the extreme.) At first we were HARRIED by the gang members, called names and insulted, but later it became a HARROWING experience as they chased and threatened us with knives.

APTITUDE
(ap TUH tude)
capacity for learning;
natural ability
Link: **ALTITUDE**

"Birds have an APTITUDE for ALTITUDE."

❑ Chris has had a champion's APTITUDE for tennis since she was four years old.

❑ Jess is all thumbs and has no APTITUDE for fixing things around the house.

❑ The APTITUDE of flora and fauna to adapt to changing environmental conditions is absolutely marvelous.

ENDURE

(in DUR)

to carry on through despite hardships; to put up with

Link: **MANURE**

"Cowboys ENDURE a lot of MANURE."

- ❑ Settlers in the 1800s ENDURED many hardships on their way to California.

- ❑ "I can't ENDURE the solitude," Jimbo Marks told his lawyer, as the sheriff placed him in an isolation cell awaiting trial.

- ❑ The ENDURING quality I recall most with loving memory about my Aunt Emma was that she never had a bad word to say about anyone.

CHRONIC
(KRAHN ik)
continuing for a long time;
continuous

Link: **RON'S HIC**

"RON'S HICcups were CHRONIC."

- ❑ George was a CHRONIC complainer, he never saw the positive side of anything.

- ❑ When lower back pain becomes CHRONIC, it's time to see a doctor.

- ❑ Her CHRONIC gossiping led to her being kicked out of the garden club.

GIDDY
(GEDD ee)
a light-headed sensation;
dizzy, frivolous
Link: CITY

*"Farmer John gets a little GIDDY
every time he goes to the CITY."*

- ❑ After Sue Ellen won the beauty contest, she was absolutely GIDDY with joy.

- ❑ Jackie didn't faint, but she said the sun was so hot she felt GIDDY.

- ❑ Bill never had more than one beer; anything more made him GIDDY.

IRASCIBLE
(i RAS uh bul)
easily angered, irritable
Link: **WRESTLE BULLS**

*"When he became IRASCIBLE, the Masked Marvel
would WRESTLE BULLS."*

❑ Normally, Rose was a pleasant wife and mother
but if a member of her family prevented her from
watching her favorite "soaps," she could become
quite IRASCIBLE.

❑ Uncle Tim was a real grouch, even on his birthday
he would find a way to become as IRASCIBLE as
a spoiled child.

❑ The school principal became so IRASCIBLE even
his teachers avoided speaking to him.

COWER
(KOW ur)
cringe from fear; to shrink away

Link: COW

"Bessie, the COWERING COW, never could stand the sight of her own milk."

- When Sheriff Wild Bill Hickok entered the Last Chance Saloon, the villains COWERED in fear.

- The sound of the rusty door opening in the middle of the night made Sue COWER behind her bed.

- Jack COWERED in frustration just to think about coming home from vacation and finding all the homework he had to catch up on.

GOSSAMER
(GOSS uh mer)
delicate floating cobwebs; a sheer gauzy
fabric; something delicate, light, flimsy
Link: CUSTOMER

*"The spider's GOSSAMER captured many
unhappy CUSTOMERS."*

❑ The bride wore a white silk wedding dress which
touched the floor as she proceeded up the aisle to
the altar. A GOSSAMER of fine Italian lace gently
touched her face.

❑ Between the audience and the actors on the stage
hung a thin GOSSAMER of fabric, heightening the
feeling that the actors were in a dream-like setting.

QUEUE
(Q)
to form or to wait in line
Link: Q

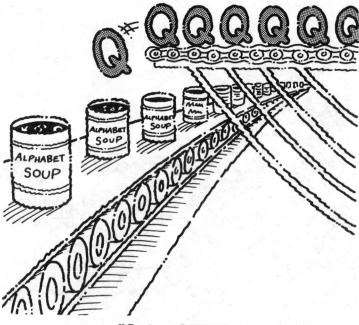

"Qs in a QUEUE."

❑ During the Wimbledon Tennis Championships, fans QUEUE outside the gates the day before and spend the night waiting for the gates to open the following morning.

❑ The sisters decided not to attend the movie because a line was QUEUING up as they arrived, and they didn't want to stand in a QUEUE in the cold, night air.

REVIEW #5: Match the word with its definition.

1. laconic - (tonic)
2. harrowing - (hare rowing)
3. aptitude - (altitude)
4. endure - (manure)
5. chronic - (Ron's hic)
6. giddy - (city)
7. irascible - (wrestle bulls)
8. cower - (cow)
9. gossamer - (customer)
10. queue - (q)

a. natural ability
b. continuous
c. something delicate
d. using few words
e. easily angered
f. to cringe from fear
g. wait in line
h. dizzy, light-headed
i. put up with hardships
j. disturbing, frightening

Fill in the blanks with the appropriate word. The word form may need changing.

1. The spider's _____ trapped many unhappy customers.

2. After a _____ escape from a shark attack, Eddie vowed never to dive again.

3. Birds have an _____ for altitude.

4. During the Wimbledon Tennis Championships, fans _____ outside the gates the day before it starts.

5. The doctor was _____ with his patients to the point of being rude.

6. When Sheriff Wild Bill Hickok entered the Last Chance Saloon, the villains _____ in fear.

7. When lower back pain becomes _____, it's time to see a doctor.

8. Farmer John gets a little _____ every time he goes to the city.

9. The school principal became so _____ even his teachers avoided speaking to him.

10. Settlers in the 1800s _____ many hardships on their way to California.

69

MYRIAD
(MIR ee ud)
an extremely large number
Link: **MIRROR ADD**

*"Many MIRRORS ADD a MYRIAD
of reflections."*

❑ George was a hypochondriac, weighted down by
MYRIAD concerns about his health.

❑ On a clear night in Alaska the sky is filled with a
MYRIAD of stars.

❑ Jane said she had a MYRIAD of things to do to get
ready for the party.

ACCOLADE
(AK uh layd)
an award, an honor;
approval, praise
Link: LEMONADE

*"Jane and Jack received ACCOLADES
for their LEMONADE."*

❑ The ACCOLADES given our chemistry teacher as the teacher of the year were nothing compared to the ACCOLADES her students gave her when she accidentally blew up the lab and class was cancelled for the remainder of the term.

❑ The ACCOLADES she received for making the Olympic Swim Team quickly went to her head, and she thought she was grand madam of the swimming pool.

GRANDILOQUENT

(gran DIL uh kwunt)
attempting to impress with big
words or grand gestures
Link: **GRAND ELEPHANT**

*"The GRAND ELEPHANT made a
GRANDILOQUENT speech."*

❑ It was another GRANDILOQUENT political af-
fair; the candidates made the same old promises
for lower taxes and more free services.

❑ They may be eloquent, but there is nothing grand
about pompous GRANDILOQUENT speakers.

❑ The new teacher's GRANDILOQUENCE didn't
fool the class one bit. She really knew very little
about South American history.

CAUCUS
(KAW kus)
a meeting of the members of a political party to make decisions; to assemble in or hold a caucus
Link: CACTUS

"A CACTUS CAUCUS."

❑ A CAUCUS was held by the members of the delegation to determine if they should hold a special CAUCUS for the unmarried members.

❑ Some delegates to political conventions are selected in CAUCUSES, while others are appointed.

DROMEDARY
(DRO me dary)
a one-humped domesticated camel
Link: **ROAMING DAIRY**

*"On the Arabian deserts, a mother DROMEDARY
is a ROAMING DAIRY."*

❑ The DROMEDARY is widely used as a beast of burden in Northern Africa and Western Asia.

❑ A DROMEDARY is also known as an Arabian camel.

74

DEMONIC
(dee MON ik)
one who works devilishly (a demon for work), a
persistent person, force or drive; an evil person
Link: **DEMON**

*"Professor Luke E. Fer was a DEMONIC DEMON
when it came time for his final exams."*

❑ Walter had a DEMONIC approach to business, he
was only out there for himself and the money.

❑ In pursuit of an OLYMPIC medal, Jack's practice
habits were DEMONIC; six hours a day on the
track was his norm.

❑ To have a DEMONIC attitude in attempting to
achieve your goals will sooner or later payoff.

NOXIOUS
(KNOCKS ee us)
physically or mentally destructive,
or harmful to human beings
Link: **KNOCKS US**

*"Her cheap perfume was so NOXIOUS, it
almost KNOCKED US out."*

❑ The NOXIOUS pollutants discharged into the bay
by the paper mill killed all the marine life.

❑ It is NOXIOUS to live in big city surroundings if
you love spacious, outdoor country-living.

❑ (OBNOXIOUS is to be exposed to something
NOXIOUS.) Jenny's flirtatious behavior with her
best friend's husband was OBNOXIOUS.

PROFICIENT
(pruh FISH unt)
skillful; to be very good at
something
Link: **PRO FISHERMAN**

"The ultimate PROFICIENT PRO FISHERMAN."

❑ Wally was the most competent, PROFICIENT ice skater in our league, but he wasn't good enough to make the Olympic team.

❑ June was so PROFICIENT as executive secretary, she was promoted and became vice president of sales.

77

HARANGUE
(huh RANG)
to lecture, berate; a long
bombastic speech
Link: **MERINGUE**

"The mayor's HARANGUE that women should stay home more was met with MERINGUE pies."

- ❑ Our sergeant HARANGUED the recruits for not keeping in step as the platoon practiced marching.

- ❑ Our neighbor is a farmer who goes to town once a week on Saturdays and HARANGUES everyone he meets on how bad the government treats farmers.

- ❑ A perpetual HARANGUER, Jeannie was a feminist who believed everyone who didn't believe as she did was an anti-feminist.

ATROPHY
(AT ruh fee)
to wither away
Link: **TROPHY**

*"Once a TROPHY champion, Jim's muscles
ATROPHIED due to a chronic illness."*

- ❏ The author's interest in writing ATROPHIED after he won the Pulitzer Prize for literature.

- ❏ The ATROPHIC condition of the mummy was apparent as soon as the tomb was opened.

- ❏ The ATROPHYING state of the starving children left no doubt that the rescue mission had arrived just in time.

REVIEW #6: Match the word with its definition.

1. myriad - (mirror)
2. accolade - (lemonade)
3. grandiloquent - (grand elephant)
4. caucus - (cactus)
5. dromedary - (roaming dairy)
6. demonic - (demon)
7. noxious - (knocks us)
8. proficient - (pro fisherman)
9. harangue - (meringue)
10. atrophy - (trophy)

a. to berate; lecture
b. to wither away
c. impress with words
d. demon for work
e. domesticated camel
f. large number
g. meeting, to assemble
h. praise
i. skillful
j. harmful

Fill in the blanks with the appropriate word. The word form may need changing.

1. A _____ is also known as an Arabian camel.

2. Walter had a _____ approach to business, he worked seven days a week and twice on holidays.

3. The author's interest in writing _____ after he won the Pulitzer Prize for literature.

4. Our sergeant _____ the recruits for not keeping in step while the platoon practiced marching.

5. The _____ pollutants discharged into the bay by the paper mill killed all the marine life.

6. They may be eloquent, but there is nothing grand about pompous _____ speakers.

7. Delegates to political conventions are selected in _____, while others are appointed.

8. Jane said she had a _____ of things to do to get ready for the party.

9. The _____ she received for making the Olympic Team quickly went to her head.

10. Wally was the most competent, _____ ice skater in our league.

CATAPULT
(CAT uh pult)
slingshot
Link: **CAT**

"Testing the first CAT CATAPULT."

❑ When the Dolphins beat the Steelers, the victory CATAPULTED them into first place.

❑ The Atlas entry won at Indianapolis by drafting behind the lead car and CATAPULTING forward to take the lead at the finish line.

❑ Before the invention of cannons, CATAPULTS were used by armies to attack castles and forts.

GLUTTON
(GLUT en)
one who eats or consumes a great deal; having capacity to receive or withstand something

Link: **GUT TON**

*"If you're a GLUTTON, your
GUT could weigh a TON."*

- ❑ Every day at school lunch the Pitts children behave in a GLUTTONOUS manner, so much so, it made one wonder if they were ever fed at home.

- ❑ Jack was a GLUTTON for punishment; no matter how many times he was knocked down in the fight, he kept getting up.

- ❑ A baseball freak, JoAnne GLUTTONOUSLY reads every sports book on baseball she can get her hands on.

MUSTER
(MUS tur)
to collect or gather; the act of
inspection or critical examination
Link: MUSTARD

*"Each morning the MUSTARD troops
are MUSTERED for roll call."*

❑ In 1836 the Texans at the Alamo MUSTERED all the troops available to defend against the invading Mexican Army.

❑ The restaurant owner inspected the kitchen and said the eating utensils did not pass MUSTER, and for the dish washer to wash them all over again.

❑ He was MUSTERED into the army at the age of eighteen.

BEGET
(bi GET)
to give birth to; to create
Link: **FORGET**

"The old lady who lived in the shoe BEGAT so many children she would FORGET who was who."

- ❑ Prior to the development of large farm machinery, farmers used to BEGET large families to help them run their farms.

- ❑ Chronic lying becomes a habit which starts out with one small lie, which BEGETS a second lie, which BEGETS a third lie, and so on.

- ❑ The Wright brothers didn't invent the airplane, but they were the BEGETTERS of the first sustained flight in the United States.

CURTAIL

(ker TALE)

to truncate or abridge; to lessen,
usually by cutting away from

Link: **CAT TAIL**

*"Rex readies himself to CURTAIL
the CAT'S TAIL."*

- ❏ The chairman requested that we should CURTAIL any further discussion of women's rights until the women arrived.

- ❏ Sheriff McDougall CURTAILED all further night patrols east of the river until bullet-proof windows were installed in his patrol cars.

- ❏ The factory bosses CURTAILED the employment of any more workers until the strike was over.

PARANOIA

(par uh NOY uh)

a mental illness of unreasonable anxiety, especially believing someone is out to get you, or that you are an important person

Link: **DESTROY 'YA**

"PARANOIA will DESTROY 'YA."

- ❑ Julie's PARANOIA was so advanced she thought everyone who came to her door was an assassin who had come to kill her.

- ❑ (A person suffering from PARANOIA is said to be PARANOID.) Joshua was absolutely PARANOID about walking under a ladder.

- ❑ When Ramon told his wife she was PARANOID about her hair, he meant she was very sensitive to criticism.

FACILITATE
(fuh SILL uh tate)
to make easier, to help bring about
Link: CELL MATE

*"You're lucky to have a CELL MATE who
FACILITATES a homey atmosphere."*

❑ Cassette tapes FACILITATE learning a foreign
language.

❑ In order to FACILITATE the sale of their home,
George came down on the price.

❑ Jack's tools FACILITATED the repair of the sink.

CRAVEN
(KRA ven)
cowardly
Link: **RAVEN**

"A CRAVEN RAVEN on the run."

❑ The soldier was full of bluster about how bravely he would fight, but his comrades later found him to be CRAVEN once the battle started.

❑ To let his wife do his fighting for him was the act of a CRAVEN husband with no backbone.

❑ The CRAVENLY act of the assassin, John Wilkes Booth, led to the death of President Lincoln.

MODE
(mowed)
a way or method of doing something;
type, manner, fashion
Link: **TOAD**

*"TOADS have a special MODE
for catching dinner."*

- Four-wheel drive vehicles have gears to go from two- to four-wheel drive MODE.

- Once he became a lawyer, Hal put aside his jeans and dressed in the MODE of his contemporaries, conservative dark suits, white shirts and ties.

- Our vacation was in a laid-back MODE, sleeping-in late and then catching rays on the beach.

ALIENATE
(AY lee uh nayt)
to make hostile; to cause to feel
unwelcome or estranged
Link: **ALIEN ATE**

*"The chief ALIEN ATE all the ice cream
and ALIENATED his crew."*

- ❑ Her boss ALIENATED his secretary by shouting at her when she made a mistake.

- ❑ All during school, Bob Smith felt ALIENATED by the other students because he wore his hair down to his knees.

- ❑ Barb was ALIENATED from her group when they learned that she was the town gossip.

REVIEW #7: Match the word with its definition.

1. catapult - (cat)
2. glutton - (gut ton)
3. muster - (mustard)
4. beget - (forget)
5. curtail - (cat tail)
6. paranoia - (destroy 'ya)
7. facilitate - (cell mate)
8. craven - (raven)
9. mode - (toad)
10. alienate - (alien ate)

a. mental illness
b. give birth to
c. consume a great deal
d. cowardly
e. collect, inspect
f. to make hostile
g. manner, fashion
h. to make easier
i. to lessen, shorten
j. slingshot

Fill in the blanks with the appropriate word. The word form may need changing.

1. The Texans _____ all the troops to defend the Alamo.

2. Jack was a _____ for punishment.

3. Before the invention of cannons, _____ were used by armies to attack castles and forts.

4. In order to _____ the sale of their home, George came down on the price.

5. Toads have a special _____ for catching dinner.

6. The chief alien ate all the ice cream and _____ his crew.

7. Julie's _____ was so advanced she thought everyone who came to her door was going to kill her.

8. The old lady who lived in the shoe _____ so many children she would forget who was who.

9. The chairman requested that we should _____ any further discussion of women's rights until the women arrived.

10. John Wilkes Booths' _____ act led to the death of President Lincoln.

91

OBTUSE
(ob tuse)
insensitive; block-headed,
slow in comprehension
Link: **NOOSE**

*"Don't be OBTUSE, the horse-thief gets the
NOOSE, not the horse."*

- ❑ Hazel was so OBTUSE she thought a watched pot of water never boils.

- ❑ The OBTUSENESS of some people is due to their unwillingness to accept new ideas.

- ❑ Don't pretend to be so OBTUSE. You know the idea of business investing is to buy low and sell high.

SCRUTINIZE
(SKROOT uh nyze)
to look very carefully; to examine
Link: **SCREW EYES**

"U.S. Customs officials have SCREW EYES when they SCRUTINIZE baggage."

❑ Newspaper proof readers SCRUTINIZE an entire newspaper each day.

❑ Each soldier's uniform is SCRUTINIZED by his commanding officer.

❑ I SCRUTINIZED all the books in the library and found several I had wanted.

CONGENIAL

(kun JEAN ee ul)
pleasant to be around;
social, agreeable

Link: **JEANS**

"Folks in JEANS are very CONGENIAL."

☐ Dr. Armstrong was very CONGENIAL, always a smile and a kind word for his patients, and candies for the children.

☐ Miss Florida was voted Miss CONGENIALITY in the Miss America pageant.

☐ The atmosphere at the property appraiser's office is CONGENIAL. Everyone enjoys their job, and visitors are welcome at any time.

FJORD
(fyord)
a long narrow inlet from the sea
between steep cliffs or hills
Link: FORD

"FORDS in a FJORD."

❑ Norway and New Zealand are two countries noted for having the most scenic FJORDS in the world.

❑ FJORDS are generally deep so that large cruise ships have more than enough water to navigate up their length.

❑ The Grand Canyon could be the grandest FJORD of all, if only it were on the coast with an inlet from the sea.

ASPIRE
(ass PIRE)
something one hopes to achieve; goal
Link: **RETIRE**

*"Jim ASPIRED to RETIRE early and
become a man of leisure."*

- ❑ Tim ASPIRED to be the valedictorian of his class at graduation and studied hard to reach that goal.

- ❑ The counselor told Jim's parents that his problem in school was he didn't ASPIRE for anything. He had no goals or career direction.

- ❑ As a young child, General Custer had ASPIRED to become a musician, but later decided to become a general instead.

MARTYR

(MAHR tur)

someone willing to sacrifice and even give
his/her life for a cause; also one who
pretends suffering to gain sympathy

Link: **HARDER**

"It's HARDER to be a MARTYR."

☐ She was a professional MARTYR, all-suffering for
her children, or so she would tell them ten times a
day.

☐ Joan of Arc was undoubtedly the most famous
MARTYR in modern history, burned at the stake
because she refused to go against her beliefs.

☐ Jack was a MARTYR to his job; he worked seven
days a week and rarely took a day off.

CITADEL

(SIT uh dul)
a fortress overlooking a city;
a stronghold

Link: SIT WELL

*"It pays to SIT WELL on the edge
of a CITADEL."*

❑ Charlie was a CITADEL of strength, always there
for you no matter what.

❑ West Point is considered a CITADEL of military
learning, a fact easily understood when you come
to understand that most generals attended West
Point.

❑ There are many ancient CITADELS in Spain; they
are among the attractions most visited by tourists.

DOLDRUMS
(DOHL drums)
a period or condition of
depression or inactivity
Link: DOLL DRUMS

*"All covered with dust, the DOLL DRUMS
were in the DOLDRUMS."*

- Ever since Jackie's dog died, the little fellow has not touched his toys, moping around day after day in the DOLDRUMS.

- For thirteen days we were becalmed in the Horse Latitudes near the equator, our ship drifting in the DOLDRUMS without the faintest breeze to fill the sails of our vessel.

CONSENSUS
(kun SEN sus)
general agreement

Link: **SENDS US**

"We are in CONSENSUS, this guy SENDS US."

- ❑ After taking a CONSENSUS of the congressmen present, the bill to legalize nude beaches failed to pass.

- ❑ The CONSENSUS of the faculty was that no more chili dogs were to be served at the school lunch.

- ❑ A CONSENSUS is more than a majority, it means most everyone agrees.

BLATHER
(BLAH thur)
to talk nonsensically
Link: <u>LATHER</u>

"Karen and Allison BLATHERED until their mouths LATHERED."

❑ Everything the media reported about the supposed plane disaster never happened. It was a bunch of BLATHER by uninformed journalists.

❑ Children have great imaginations, and often BLATHER about ghosts that supposedly enter their rooms and either scare them or play with them.

REVIEW #8: Match the word with its definition.

1. obtuse - (noose)
2. scrutinize - (screw eyes)
3. congenial - (jeans)
4. fjord - (Ford)
5. aspire - (retire)
6. martyr - (harder)
7. citadel - (sit well)
8. doldrums - (doll drums)
9. consensus - (sends us)
10. blather - (lather)

a. general agreement
b. a fortress
c. period of inactivity
d. pleasant, social
e. to talk nonsensical
f. narrow sea inlet
g. hopeful goal
h. to look over carefully
i. block-headed
j. one who sacrifices

Fill in the blanks with the appropriate word. The word form may need changing.

1. Richard Petty always likes to _____ his car before a race.

2. Jack was a _____ to his job; he worked seven days a week and rarely took a day of.

3. Children have great imaginations, and often _____ about ghosts and goblins.

4. Ever since Jack's dog died, he just mopes around the house, day after day in the _____.

5. There are many ancient _____ in Spain; they are among the attractions most visited by tourists.

6. The _____ of the faculty was that no more chili dogs were to be served at the school lunch.

7. Jim _____ to retire early and become a man of leisure.

8. Hazel was so _____ she thought a watched pot of water never boils.

9. Norway and New Zealand are two countries noted for having the most scenic _____ in the world.

10. Dr. Armstrong was very _____, with always a smile and a kind word for his patients.

102

DEFAME

(di FAYME)
to libel or slander; take
away a good name

Link: RENAME

"When the good name of William Bonney was DEFAMED, reporters RENAMED him 'Billy the Kid'."

- ☐ DEFAMED and defeated, Napoleon was exiled to the Island of Elba.

- ☐ False accusations have DEFAMED the reputations of many fair ladies by unscrupulous, lying men.

- ☐ Thomas Jefferson was once quoted as saying, "DEFAMATION is becoming a way of life insomuch that a dish of tea cannot be digested without the stimulant."

CURVILINEAR
(kurv ah LIN ee ur)
formed, bound, or characterized
by curved lines
Link: **CURVY LINES**

*"The skater's CURVY LINES outlined her
CURVILINEAR skating program."*

❑ Squares and rectangles have no CURVILINEAR
lines.

❑ Surveyors have special instruments to lay out
CURVILINEAR streets in subdivisions.

ELAPSE
(ee LAPS)
to pass or go by (said of time)
Link: **COLLAPSE**

"Ted ran the mile in the ELAPSED time of three minutes, forty-seven seconds, and then COLLAPSED."

❑ Time ELAPSES slowly when someone is waiting for important news.

❑ Two years ELAPSED before they were to meet again, but all the time Jonathan knew Annette was the girl he was going to marry.

❑ During World War II, the siege of Stalingrad lasted five months; in the ELAPSING battle 750,000 Russians and 400,000 Germans died.

VEER

(ve ur)

change in direction

Link: **PIER**

*"Vern, I told you to VEER
at the end of the PIER."*

☐ When you arrive at the castle, VEER left around the wall and follow the foot trail until you come to the valley.

☐ Without warning, Flight #638 suddenly VEERED off the runway and slammed into a small plane parked outside the hanger. Fortunately no one was seriously hurt.

☐ Arthur never VEERED from the path of honor and dignity.

KARMA
(KAHR muh)
fate, destiny; to detect good or bad vibrations
from something or someone
Link: **HARM-A**

"No HARM-A will come if you have good KARMA."

- ☐ All his life he possessed a protective KARMA that kept him out of harm's way.

- ☐ Louise often told her friends it was her KARMA to die young and beautiful.

- ☐ Genghis Khan emanated a KARMA of death and destruction.

ASTUTE
(uh STOOT)
quick in discernment; shrewd,
clever, keen
Link: **SUIT**

*"Larry thought a new SUIT would make him appear
more ASTUTE for his job interview."*

- ❑ Louisa has a natural ASTUTENESS in dealing with angry people and winning them over to her view, thereby settling matters amicably.

- ❑ Like many gamblers, John thought he was very ASTUTE when it came to betting on horses. Only his wife kept telling him if he was so ASTUTE, he would realize he lost more often than he won.

- ❑ Mary was known to be very ASTUTE. She was always the first to finish her assignments.

MISNOMER
(miss NO mur)
an incorrect or inappropriate name
Link: **MISS HOMER**

*"What a MISNOMER, our little MISS HOMER
struck out five times in a row."*

❑ A nickname like "Speedy" is a MISNOMER when
directed toward one who is slow at what they do.

❑ We usually have dinner at this very small Italian
restaurant called The Spaghetti Factory, obviously
a MISNOMER of major proportions.

❑ It was no MISNOMER when they called Harry
Houdini, "The Great Houdini," as he was the
greatest escape artist of his time.

RESURGENT

(re sur jent)

a rise after defeat

Link: SERGEANT

"A RESURGENT SERGEANT."

- After losing last year, the RESURGENT Frank Morrow said he was going to run for class president.

- The RESURGENT little boy was determined to ride his bike without training wheels.

- RESURGENCE and strong determination helps most climbers conquer Mount Everest.

ARTISAN
(AHRT uh sun)
a worker skilled in a craft
Link: **ART IN SAND**

"Little Jimmy was a SAND CASTLE ARTISAN."

- ❏ The ARTISANS of Pueblo, Mexico are known for their beautiful pottery.

- ❏ The ARTISANS arrived early in the morning to repaint and landscape the house.

- ❏ The Italian painter and sculptor Michelangelo was both an artist and an ARTISAN.

DRACONIAN
(dray KOH nee un)
hard, severe, cruel
Link: **DRACULA**

"Count DRACULA often behaved in a DRACONIAN manner."

- ❑ Mr. Jeb had a DRACONIAN personality. Nothing his students did pleased him, and rarely did half of his students get passing grades.

- ❑ Judge McNamara handed down a DRACONIAN sentence to the defendant, sixty days for littering.

- ❑ The word DRACONIAN did not originate with the fictional character, Count Dracula, but with an ancient Greek official named Dracula who created a harsh code of laws.

REVIEW #9: Match the word with its definition.

1. defame - (rename)
2. curvilinear - (curvy lines)
3. elapse - (collapse)
4. veer - (pier)
5. karma - (harm-a)
6. astute - (suit)
7. misnomer - (Miss Homer)
8. resurgent - (sergeant)
9. artisan - (art in sand)
10. draconian - (Dracula)

a. passage of time
b. curved lines
c. shrewd, clever
d. rise after defeat
e. libel or slander
f. change direction
g. skilled worker
h. severe, cruel
i. fate, destiny
j. inappropriate name

Fill in the blanks with the appropriate word. The word form may need changing.

1. Surveyors have special instruments to lay out _____ streets in subdivisions.

2. All his life he possessed a protective _____ that kept him out of harm's way.

3. Larry thought a new suit would make him appear _____ for his job interview.

4. Mr. Jeb had a _____ personality. Nothing his students did pleased him and rarely did they pass.

5. The Italian painter and sculptor Michelangelo was both an artist and an _____.

6. The _____ little boy was determined to ride his bike without training wheels.

7. _____ and defeated, Napoleon was exiled to the Island of Elba.

8. Time _____ slowly when someone is awaiting important news.

9. Arthur never _____ from the path of honor and dignity.

10. Nicknames like "Speedy" are _____ when directed towards those who are really slow at what they do.

AMENABLE
(ah MEE nuh bul)
agreeable, responsible to authority, pleasant,
willing to give in to the wishes of another
Link: **MEAN BULL**

*"The matador tried to be AMENABLE
to the MEAN BULL."*

❑ Jack was such a classy guy, always AMENABLE to
any reasonable solution to a problem.

❑ The Seminole Indians were AMENABLE to our
sharing revenue from the games at their bingo hall.

❑ Jane was AMENABLE to calling back tomorrow
when the main office would be open.

PRECARIOUS
(pruh KA REE us)
unsafe, unsteady, unstable
Link: CARRY US

"To escape the dinosaur, Mississippi Jones CARRIED US to safety across a PRECARIOUS bridge."

❏ It was a PRECARIOUS moment; we were out of town, without any money and without any gas.

❏ The PRECARIOUSNESS of their situation did not fully strike the fishermen until their small boat arrived at the dock only moments before the storm struck.

❏ Isabel's habit of arriving at work late almost every morning made her job future PRECARIOUSLY uncertain.

CRITERION
(kry TEER ee un)
a standard or rule by which something
can be judged; a basis for judgment
Link: **LIBRARIAN**

*"A CRITERION for any LIBRARIAN is that she
must know how to read."*

❏ There is no special CRITERION for making a
fortune, but some say the fastest way is to marry
rich.

❏ (CRITERION is singular. CRITERIA is plural.)
The physical CRITERIA for a good basketball
player are to be seven feet tall and jump like a
kangaroo.

GUISE
(gyze)
appearance, semblance
Link: **DISGUISE**

"A master of DISGUISE, Sherlock Holmes
concealed his real GUISE."

❑ Every night the undercover detective would enter
the toughest part of town in the GUISE of a junkie,
uncovering the identity of many drug pushers.

❑ (A false appearance can also be a GUISE.) Amy was
extremely cautious of advances made toward her
by Harold because, as she put it, he had the GUISE
of an angel, but the intentions of a devil.

LESION
(LEE zhun)
wound, injury; especially one
created by a disease
Link: **LEGION**

*"Soldiers of the French Foreign LEGION
suffering from their LESIONS."*

❑ The nurses told Crystal to keep the bandage on her knee until the LESION healed; otherwise the open sore would be prone to infection by air-borne bacteria.

❑ When a person has a LESION, even a small one that will not heal, it is time to see a doctor.

❑ Ebola is an infectious disease characterized by open LESIONS of the skin.

118

GIRD

(gyrd)

to encircle as with a belt; to
prepare as for action

Link: **HERD**

*"Curly GIRDED the HERD with
his trusty lasso."*

- ❑ Johnny's job each week of the soccer season was to GIRD the field with a line of white chalk to mark the boundaries of the playing field.

- ❑ Jack hoped he could stop the invasion of weeds from his neighbor's yard by GIRDING his lawn with a pre-emergent herbicide.

- ❑ GIRDED for action, the tanks moved forward into battle formation.

119

FETISH
(FET ish)
an object of unreasonable obsessive
reverence or attention

Link: **BRITISH**

*"The BRITISH, they say, have an
absolute FETISH for tea.*

- ❑ Her psychologist said the reason Darlene had a FETISH of washing her hands a dozen times a day was because she had a guilt complex about something in her past life, and she was trying to wash the guilt away.

- ❑ Chocolate was more than a FETISH with Mary; she had to have a chocolate fix several times a day.

DISPERSE
(dis PURS)
to scatter in various directions;
distribute widely
Link: **PURSE**

*"When the thug grabbed Dee's PURSE, all
its contents were DISPERSED."*

❏ Bonaparte DISPERSED his troops strategically all
along the mountain's ridge where they could fire
down upon the Austrian Army as it advanced up
the hill.

❏ The police arrived and DISPERSED the crowd
with threats of arrest if they did not leave the
parade grounds.

DISSOLUTION
(dis uh LOO shun)
the breaking up into parts; termination
of a legal bond or contract
Link: **SOLUTION**

*"When the heirs to the estate were unable to agree on
DISSOLUTION of their parents' home, the judge's
SOLUTION was to divide it into equal parts."*

- ❑ After his wife's death, Bill fell into a DISSOLUTE
  lifestyle, caring little for his appearance or career.

- ❑ The DISSOLUTION of the committee for fine arts
  left the matter of payment to the artists undecided.

- ❑ Nothing could prevent the DISSOLUTION of our
  fraternity, even if we were the worst on campus.

FORAGE
(FOR uj)
to search or hunt for
food and provision
Link: FOREST

*"Wild animals FORAGING for
food in the FOREST."*

❑ When the last of our provisions were gone, it was decided that two men would take our only rifle and go FORAGING for game.

❑ We FORAGED through the shed for plywood, tin sheets and boards, anything with which to board up the windows and doors before the full force of the hurricane struck.

REVIEW #10: Match the word with its definition.

1. amenable - (mean bull)
2. precarious - (carry us)
3. criterion - (librarian)
4. guise - (disguise)
5. lesion - (legion)
6. gird - (herd)
7. fetish - (British)
8. disperse - (purse)
9. dissolution - (solution)
10. forage - (forest)

a. standard for judgment
b. to break into parts
c. hunt for food
d. wound
e. pleasant, agreeable
f. distribute widely
g. unsafe, unstable
h. appearance
i. object of obsession
j. encircle, prepare

Fill in the blanks with the appropriate word. The word form may need changing.

1. A master of disguise, Sherlock Holmes concealed his real _____.

2. Johnny's job each week of the soccer season was to _____ the field with a line of white chalk.

3. Ebola is an infectious disease characterized by open _____ of the skin.

4. When the last of our provisions were gone, it was time to go into the woods and _____ for food.

5. The British, they say, have an absolute _____ for tea.

6. The police arrived and _____ the crowd with threats of arrest.

7. The _____ of the committee for fine arts left the matter of payment to the artists undecided.

8. A _____ for a librarian is that she must know how to read.

9. Jack was such a classy guy, always _____ to any reasonable solution to a problem.

10. Isabel's habit of arriving to work late almost every morning made her job future _____ uncertain.

DENOUNCE
(di NOWNS)
to condemn; to expose critically
Link: **BOUNCE**

*"The other kangaroos DENOUNCED poor Roger
when he was unable to BOUNCE."*

- ❏ As an act of conscience, the young terrorist
  DENOUNCED his fellow terrorists and confessed
  their criminal acts to the police.

- ❏ The captured soldiers were asked to DENOUNCE
  their government and join in the revolution of the
  people.

- ❏ The world was flabbergasted with the Russian
  government's DENUNCIATION of Stalin so soon
  after he died.

TORQUE

(tork)

a turning or twisting force

Link: **TURK**

*"Tommy the TURK doing his famous
TORQUE TURK dance."*

- ❑ We all took our turn, but none of my brothers or I could apply enough TORQUE to open the jar of strawberry jam.

- ❑ When the propeller broke off one side, this created a TORQUE so great it tore the engine right out of its mount.

- ❑ The wrench handle was too short to generate the TORQUE required to loosen the bolt.

FATHOM
(fa THUM)
to understand fully;
to penetrate the meaning of
Link: FAT THUMB

*"Doctors could never FATHOM the reason
for Larry's FAT THUMB."*

❑ Her friends thought they had FATHOMED the
reason Estelle applied for entrance in an all-boys
college: She never had any dates.

❑ The jury found it hard to FATHOM how the
defendant could commit such a terrible crime.

❑ (In nautical terms, FATHOM is six feet of water
depth.) We dropped anchor in four FATHOMS of
water and made plans to stay for the night.

DOCILE
(DAHS ul)
easily taught or controlled;
obedient, easy to handle
Link: FOSSIL

"A DOCILE FOSSIL."

- ❑ A desirable quality of basset hounds is that they are DOCILE, and that is why they are sought as house pets.

- ❑ Cameron was a fierce competitor on the football field, but his wife said he was a sweet, DOCILE husband.

- ❑ The baby lion's DOCILITY fooled the zoo handler into believing she wouldn't scratch or bite until she proved otherwise by chewing off part of his ear.

HOVEL
(HUV ul)
a small, miserable dwelling;
an open, low shed
Link: **SHOVEL**

"The mice's HOVEL was an old, rusted SHOVEL."

- ☐ In the famous play, *Tobacco Road*, the characters were poor tobacco farmers who live in HOVELS, shacks made of cardboard and discarded wooden boxes.

- ☐ Compared to the Summertons' palatial estate on Long Island, Jane said her apartment in the Bronx was a HOVEL.

- ☐ The HOVELS where the homeless live consist of the most squalid structures.

129

BALM
(balm)
something that soothes, heals or
comforts; an oil or ointment
Link: **PALM**

*"There's nothing like a BALMY breeze
whispering through PALM trees."*

- ❑ The nurse gave me some kind of white BALM to put on my insect bites to soothe the pain.

- ❑ It was a BALMY day, perfect for a game of golf or a trip to the beach.

- ❑ After sweating through his final exams, the sound of the bell at the end of class was a BALM to Pete's nerves.

DIVINE
(di VYNE)
to foretell a prophecy;
to infer, to guess
Link: VINE

*"How was Tarzan to DIVINE this was
the time his VINE would break?"*

- ❏ Stockbrokers make their living helping their clients DIVINE when to buy and when to sell stocks.

- ❏ When you have been a policeman for years, you can almost DIVINE when your prisoner is telling the truth as opposed to when he is lying.

- ❏ (DIVINE also means supremely pleasing.) It was a DIVINE party, and a great time was had by all.

ALTERNATIVE
(all ter na tive)
the choice between two mutually exclusive
possibilities; a situation presenting such a choice
Link: **TURN NATIVE**

*"It's an ALTERNATIVE lifestyle,
he TURNED NATIVE."*

❑ "I've had six by-pass operations," said Harry. "It's
no fun, but better than the ALTERNATIVE."

❑ The ALTERNATIVE to playing in the band was to
go out for the football team.

❑ The hikers decided there was no ALTERNATIVE;
they had to get through the pass before the rains
came.

COUNTENANCE

(KOWNT uh nanz)
a person's face, especially the expression
Link: **COUNT THE NUTS**

*"By their facial COUNTENANCE alone
it was easy to COUNT THE NUTS."*

- ❑ The submarine commander's COUNTENANCE belied his true feelings of anxiety and fear.

- ❑ John Barrymore had a magnificent series of COUNTENANCES, one for every part he played.

- ❑ (To COUNTENANCE something is to tolerate or approve of it.) The coach COUNTENANCED the players' horseplay, even though he didn't approve of it.

BADGER

(BAJ ur)

to tease, annoy, harass persistently

Link: **BADGER**

"A BADGERING BADGER."

- ❏ "Don't BADGER me," Louis said to his daughter. "I promised I'd take you to the mall, so please be patient until I finish my work."

- ❏ The school bully BADGERED Rog endlessly, until one day Rog became so provoked that he socked him in the mouth.

- ❏ BADGERING is not the most admirable quality to possess; however, it is common among teenagers who constantly BADGER their younger siblings.

REVIEW #11: Match the word with its definition.

1. denounce - (bounce)   a. understand
2. torque - (Turk)   b. condemn, expose
3. fathom - (fat thumb)   c. soothing
4. docile - (fossil)   d. choice
5. hovel - (shovel)   e. small dwelling
6. balm - (palm)   f. tease, annoy
7. divine - (vine)   g. easy to handle
8. alternative - (turn native)   h. to guess; foretell
9. countenance - (count the nuts)   i. twisting force
10. badger - (badger)   j. facial expression

Fill in the blanks with the appropriate word. The word form may need changing.

1. The other kangaroos _____ poor Roger when he was unable to bounce.

2. Doctors could never _____ the reason for Larry's fat thumb.

3. How was Tarzan to _____ this was the time his vine would break?

4. The bully _____ Rog endlessly, until Rog became so provoked that he socked him.

5. The nurse gave me some kind of white _____ to put on my insect bites to soothe the pain.

6. The submarine commander's _____ belied his true feelings of anxiety and fear.

7. The hikers decided there was no _____, they must get through the pass before the snows came.

8. The wrench handle was too short to generate the _____ required to loosen the bolt.

9. A desirable quality of basset hounds is that they are _____ house pets.

10. In the play, *Tobacco Road*, the characters are poor tobacco farmers who live in _____.

135

WANE

(wain)

to decrease gradually

Link: **RAIN**

"Snowmen WANE in the RAIN."

❑ Marilyn's interest in a new beau began to WANE when she discovered Jack had invited three other girls as his date for the junior prom.

❑ With a WANING of air in his air tank, the diver knew he had to return to the surface.

❑ A WANING interest by theater-goers prompted the theater to shut down.

FRAUGHT
(fraught)
teeming with; laden; full;
involving; accompanied by
Link: CAUGHT

*"Eric CAUGHT a boatload in
a lake FRAUGHT with fish."*

❑ The freighter was FRAUGHT with cargo.

❑ Although Mark Twain's books were FRAUGHT
with humor, they nevertheless drove home good
advice for their readers, young and old.

❑ FRAUGHT with guilt about losing her temper
with the children, Mary tried to make it up to
them by treating them to ice cream after supper.

CHASM

(KAZ um)

a deep opening in the earth's surface; a gorge;
differences of opinion, interests, loyalties

Link: SPASM

"A SPASM in the CHASM."

- ❏ "There are CHASMS and there are CHASMS,"
  said the professor. "The Grand Canyon is one big
  CHASM, but I fear some of you have CHASMS
  where your noggins ought to be."

- ❏ There was a CHASM of difference between their
  attitudes of what a marriage should consist of.

ERUDITE
(ER yoo dyte)
deeply learned, scholarly
Link: AIRTIGHT

"Knowing that his case was AIRTIGHT, the defense attorney became confident and ERUDITE."

❑ Most professional speakers are ERUDITE, with the understanding of proper grammatical structure and a large vocabulary at their command.

❑ Students who plan to go to law school take classes in speech and debate in order to become verbally ERUDITE.

❑ (To be ERUDITE is to have ERUDITION.) The extent of Dr. Smith's library is an indication of his ERUDITION.

ALSO-RAN
(AWL so ran)
one who is defeated in a race, election,
or other competition; loser
Link: AWESOME FAN

*"The tortoise was an ALSO-RAN until he
strapped on an AWESOME FAN."*

❑ Even though George Bush received millions of
votes in the presidential election, he was an ALSO-
RAN to Bill Clinton.

❑ With twenty thousand runners in the New York
Marathon, even if you defeat nineteen thousand
nine hundred and ninety eight, you would still be
an ALSO-RAN.

ELFIN
(EL fin)
small and sprightly;
mischievous, fairylike

Link: **ELEPHANT**

*"An ELFIN ELEPHANT is a strange
sight to see."*

- ❑ Jane is very small and has a magical, ELFIN charm about her until she starts to sing. Then she sounds like a bullfrog in a pond.

- ❑ The entire family had an ELFIN quality, like little people who belonged in the Land of Lilliputians.

AGGRANDIZE
(uh GRAN dyze)
to exaggerate, to cause to appear
greater in power, influence
Link: **GRAND EYES**

*"Ladies acquire GRAND EYES with mascara and false
eyelashes to AGGRANDIZE their eyes."*

❑ George was the principal **AGGRANDIZER** of his
own achievements, making the little ones bigger
and the bigger ones unbelievable. He was self-
AGGRANDIZING to the point where his boast-
fulness created a negative impression.

❑ The greatest **AGGRANDIZEMENT** of the entire
evening was when the Russian claimed that Russia
had won World War II without any help from the
United States or the other allies.

ENSEMBLE
(ahn SOM bul)
a coordinated outfit or costume;
a musical group
Link: **HANDSOME DEVIL**

*"James Bond was a HANDSOME DEVIL
in his spy ENSEMBLE."*

❑ The popular ENSEMBLE for students today is blue jeans and a T-shirt.

❑ A French fashion designer will work an entire year to get ready to show his ENSEMBLES.

❑ The wedding ENSEMBLE consisted of a troupe of gypsy musicians, dancers and singers.

TETHER
(teh thur)
a rope or chain that allows limited movement;
the limit of one's resources or strength
Link: <u>LEATHER</u>

*"Horses are TETHERED with a
rope or LEATHER strap."*

❑ Norman told the guys that he had too much work
to go camping, but we knew it was because his
wife had him TETHERED to a short leash and
wouldn't let him go.

❑ We TETHERED the boat to the dock with lines
both fore and aft.

144

CLAIMANT

(KLAY ment)
a person making a claim

Link: **CLAIM ANT**

"A CLAIMANT CLAIMING ANTS."

- ❏ The CLAIMANT of the Virginia City silver mine was Scott "Wormy" McClennahan, a miner.

- ❏ The judge awarded all six of the CLAIMANTS an equal share of the insurance money.

- ❏ Rosalie not only wanted the house in her divorce from Robert, but she was also the CLAIMANT of his doll collection.

REVIEW #12: Match the word with its definition.

1. wane - (rain)   a. defeated in a race
2. fraught - (caught)   b. decrease
3. chasm- (spasm)   c. limiting
4. erudite - (air tight)   d. person making a claim
5. also-ran - (awesome fan)   e. small, fairy-like
6. elfin - (elephant)   f. full, teeming with
7. aggrandize - (grand eyes)   g. scholarly
8. ensemble - (handsome devil)   h. a deep opening
9. tether - (leather)   i. coordinated group
10. claimant - (claim ant)   j. to exaggerate

Fill in the blanks with the appropriate word. The word form may need changing.

1. The entire family had an _____ quality, like little people who belonged in the Land of Lilliputians.

2. The judge awarded all six of the _____ an equal share of the insurance money.

3. When the air pressure in his tank began to _____, the diver knew he had to return to the surface.

4. The popular _____ for students today are blue jeans and T-shirts.

5. We _____ the boat to the dock with lines both fore and aft.

6. Ladies acquire grand eyes with mascara and false eyelashes to _____ their eyes.

7. Even though George Bush received millions of votes, he was an _____ to Bill Clinton.

8. There was a _____ of difference between their attitudes of what a marriage should consist of.

9. Students who plan to go to law school take classes in speech and debate to become verbally _____.

10. Eric caught a boatload in a lake _____ with fish.

146

ENTICE
(in TICE)
to lure, to attract, to tempt
in a pleasing fashion
Link: **MICE**

"The best kind of bait to use to ENTICE cats is MICE."

❑ The delicious aroma of a hamburger stand often ENTICES the passerby to stop for a snack.

❑ An ENTICING feature of working in a bakery is that you get to eat all the doughnuts you want.

❑ Your job proposal in Michigan is ENTICING, but my family likes it here in Palm Beach; Michigan's winters are too cold for native Floridians like us.

PHILANTHROPY

(fi LAN thruh pee)
love of mankind, especially through
charitable gifts and deeds

Link: **PHIL ANTHROPY**

*"PHIL ANTHROPY was a
PHILANTHROPIST."*

- ❑ Will Rogers was a famous PHILANTHROPIC humorist who always said he never met a man he didn't like.

- ❑ In the movie, *Good Sam*, Gary Cooper's character was so PHILANTHROPIC, giving to anyone in need and keeping so little for his own family, that his wife left him.

MISANTHROPY
(MIS an thruh pee)
someone who hates mankind
Link: **MISS ANTHROPY**

"MISS ANTHROPY was a MISANTHROPIC person."

❑ A more MISANTHROPIC person you never did see. He hates everyone.

❑ Some people live their entire lives never realizing they have a MISANTHROPIC attitude about the world, because first and foremost they have never liked themselves.

MIRAGE
(muh RAJGE)
unreal reflection; an optical
illusion
Link: **GARAGE**

*"The GARAGE they thought they saw crossing
the desert was only a MIRAGE."*

- ❑ Her beauty was mostly a MIRAGE created by the art of cosmetics.

- ❑ Desert caravans often see MIRAGES on days when the sun reflects heat waves off the burning sands.

- ❑ The MIRAGE of the lake was a welcome sight to the parched desert traveler, until he bent down to take a drink and got a mouthful of sand.

NOISOME
(NOY sum)
stinking; offensive; disgusting
Link: **ANNOY SOME**

*"Inconsiderate, NOISOME smokers are
likely to ANNOY SOME."*

- ❑ Tobacco smoke is now considered so NOISOME in the majority of public places that smoking has become off limits.

- ❑ The comedian's act was absolutely NOISOME; all of his jokes depended entirely on four-lettered vulgarities.

- ❑ When I opened the garbage can, the odor was so NOISOME I thought I might suffocate before I could get the lid back on.

COUP

(koo)

the violent overthrow of a government by a small group; a victorious accomplishment

Link: **CREW**

"In a midnight COUP, the mutinous CREW of 'The Bounty' threw Captain Bligh off his ship."

- ❑ In this century alone there have been almost one hundred military COUPS in Latin America.

- ❑ It was a real COUP for James when his teammates elected him captain of the basket weaving team.

- ❑ "What a COUP!" Rachel Reed declared when she convinced her parents to let her to go to Daytona Beach for spring break.

HOARD

(hoard)

to accumulate for future use;
stockpile

Link: **STORED**

*"A squirrel's HOARD of nuts must be STORED
for the approaching winter."*

❑ Whenever there is a hint of a gold shortage, people often HOARD the precious metal.

❑ We told Ed there was no point in his HOARDING all the cake; he might as well share with us before it spoiled.

❑ The government announced during the national crisis that HOARDERS would be punished with jail sentences.

LANGUISH

(LANG gwish)
to become weak or feeble;
sag with loss of strength
Link: **LAND FISH**

"A FISH on LAND will quickly LANGUISH."

- ❏ An outdoorsman all his life, Mr. Franklin quickly LANGUISHED in his job as a night watchman.

- ❏ It was so hot in the theater, Charlotte soon began to LANGUISH.

- ❏ (To LANGUISH is to be LANGUID.) The fish in the aquarium hardly stirred, moving LANGUIDLY when they moved at all.

CLOISTER
(KLOY stur)
a tranquil, secluded place
Link: **OYSTER**

"An OYSTER in his CLOISTER."

❏ Mary regarded her sewing room as a CLOISTER where she could withdraw from the hectic life of a mother of six and enjoy moments of privacy.

❏ (To CLOISTER someone is to place them in a place of seclusion, although they may or may not be in the company of others.) Jim CLOISTERED himself in his hotel room for the entire week of his vacation.

OUST
(owst)

to eject; to force out; to banish

Link: **HOUSE**

"The landlord OUSTED the tenant from the HOUSE when he didn't pay his rent."

❑ The people in his part of the stands wanted to have Roger OUSTED for making too much noise during the tennis match.

❑ The head referee then reported to the tournament director that an OUSTER had taken place on court number one.

❑ Later, after Roger's OUSTER by the ushers, he complained to the management that he should be allowed to cheer anytime he wanted.

REVIEW #13: Match the word with its definition.

1. entice - (mice)
2. philanthropy - (Phil Anthropy)
3. misanthropy - (Miss Anthropy)
4. mirage - (garage)
5. noisome - (annoy some)
6. coup - (crew)
7. hoard - (stored)
8. languish - (land fish)
9. cloister - (oyster)
10. oust - (house)

a. loves mankind
b. to lure, attract
c. accumulate, store
d. offensive
e. hates mankind
f. eject, force out
g. optical illusion
h. violent overthrow
i. become weak
j. secluded place

Fill in the blanks with the appropriate word. The word form may need changing.

1. The landlord _____ the tenant from the house.

2. Desert caravans often see _____ on days when the sun reflects heat waves off the burning sands.

3. Will Rogers was a famous _____ humorist who said he never met a man he didn't like.

4. The best kind of bait to use to _____ cats is mice.

5. A squirrel's _____ of nuts must be stored for the approaching winter.

6. In this century alone there have been almost one hundred military _____ in Latin America.

7. Mary regarded her sewing room as a _____ where she could withdraw from her hectic life.

8. Tobacco smoke is now considered so _____ in the majority of public places.

9. It was so hot in the theater, Charlotte soon began to _____.

10. A more _____ person you never did see. He hates everyone.

157

CREDITOR
(KRED uh tor)
a person to whom money is owed
Link: **PREDATOR**

"Beware the CREDITOR who is a PREDATOR."

❑ Mr. Randolph's lawyer recommended he declare bankruptcy; he had too many CREDITORS and not enough assets with which to pay.

❑ The entire banking industry is based entirely on performing as a CREDITOR for depositors, then turning around and becoming CREDITORS for borrowers.

❑ Anyone who has CREDIT also has a CREDITOR.

PILLAGE
(PIL luhge)
to rob of goods by violent seizure,
plunder; to take as spoils
Link: **VILLAGE**

*"Blackbeard the Pirate gives last minute orders before
his crew PILLAGES the VILLAGE."*

- ❑ The enemy invaders PILLAGED the village, taking everything not tied down and killing the cows and chickens.

- ❑ After the kids and their school friends PILLAGED the refrigerator, there was nothing left but a little catsup and mustard.

159

ANTECEDENT

(an tuh SEED unt)
going before; preceding; an occurrence
or event preceding another
Link: **HAND SEED**

*"The HAND that plants the SEED is the
ANTECEDENT to the hand that picks the flower."*

☐ The steam engine was the ANTECEDENT to the
gasoline engine.

☐ Your ancestors were your ANTECEDENTS.

☐ The atomic bomb was the ANTECEDENT to the
hydrogen bomb.

EMBODY
(em BAH dee)
to give bodily form to; to personify;
to make part of a system
Link: BODY

*"Jimmy sculpted a statue with the likeness of his face,
but which EMBODIED a BODY he'd never have."*

- ☐ Virginia Satir was a wonderful therapist who
  EMBODIED in her own life the loving principles
  she taught to her students.

- ☐ The EMBODIMENT of basic Christian virtues is
  to be found in the Boy Scouts' oath every scout
  must take to become a member.

161

VERBATIM

(VER bay tym)
using exactly the same words,
word for word

Link: **VERN'S BAT**

*"VERN wrote his coach's batting instructions
VERBATIM on his BAT."*

❑ The coach called the team together and said from that moment on, every player who wanted to stay on the team had to obey his rules VERBATIM.

❑ The witness told the judge he couldn't recite what the accused had said VERBATIM, but the essence of what he said was he thought the police were "on the take."

TRUNCATE
(TRUNK kate)
to shorten by cutting off
Link: **TRUNK CUT**

"The lumberjack TRUNCATED the tree when he CUT the TRUNK halfway to the top."

❑ Observing that his listeners were falling asleep, the president TRUNCATED his speech so everyone could go home.

❑ Because of unforeseen circumstances, our vacation was TRUNCATED after the first week.

❑ We TRUNCATED the brush around our house so we could have a better view of the lake.

REMORSE

(re MORSE)
a strong feeling of sadness or guilt for
having done something wrong

Link: __HORSE__

"Even HORSES feel REMORSE."

❑ John refused to feel any REMORSE for what he considered the right thing to do.

❑ The REMORSE we feel for hurting those we love is the beginning of being able to say we're sorry.

❑ When the pall bearers came forward with the casket, the wife let out a REMORSEFUL sob.

FORSAKE
(for SAYK)
to abandon, to give up,
to renounce
Link: FOUR SNAKES

"The Higgins family wisely decided to FORSAKE their campsite in favor of FOUR SNAKES."

☐ The parents urged their daughter to FORSAKE her life as a model and return to their home to become a school teacher.

☐ All the general's troops had FORSAKEN him, and he had no choice but to follow them and return to safe ground.

DEFT

(deft)

dexterous, skillful

Link: **DEAF**

"The DEAF are DEFT at reading lips."

- ❑ The quarterback DEFTLY avoided the linebacker's rush while calmly throwing a touchdown pass.

- ❑ In one DEFT move, the policeman subdued the thief and took him to the ground.

- ❑ The magician was so DEFT with a pack of cards that he could deal off the bottom with everyone watching, and no one was the wiser.

UBIQUITOUS
(yoo BIK woh tus)
the quality of being everywhere
(or seeming to) at the same time
Link: **BIG AS US**

"When you're as BIG AS US you feel UBIQUITOUS."

❑ Computers were once rare, but today are more UBIQUITOUS than typewriters.

❑ The UBIQUITY of fast-food restaurants around the world has become an established fact.

❑ Cowboy boots are as UBIQUITOUS as blue jeans at a rodeo.

REVIEW #14: Match the word with its definition.

1. creditor - (predator)
2. pillage - (village)
3. antecedent - (hand seed)
4. embody - (body)
5. verbatim - (Vern's bat)
6. truncate - (trunk cut)
7. remorse - (horse)
8. forsake - (four snakes)
9. deft - (deaf)
10. ubiquitous - (big as us)

a. being everywhere
b. to shorten
c. owed money
d. rob, plunder
e. skillful
f. feeling of guilt
g. the same words
h. give bodily form
i. to abandon
j. going before

Fill in the blanks with the appropriate word. The word form may need changing.

1. The quarterback _____ avoided the linebacker's rush while calmly throwing a touchdown pass.

2. The hand that plants the seed is the _____ to the hand that picks the flower.

3. Mr. Randolph's lawyer recommended he declare bankruptcy; he had too many _____.

4. Any player who wanted to stay on the team had to obey the coaches rules _____.

5. Because of unforeseen circumstances, our planned two week vacation was _____ to one week.

6. When you're as big as us you feel _____.

7. John refused to feel any _____ for what he considered the right thing to do.

8. The parents urged their daughter to _____ her life as a model and return home to become a teacher.

9. Virginia Satir was a wonderful therapist who _____ in her own life the loving principles she taught to her students.

10. The enemy invaders _____ the village, taking everything not tied down.

INSOUCIANT
(in SOO see unt)
calm and carefree; lighthearted
Link: SOUTH SEA ANT

*"SOUTH SEA ANTS are the most
INSOUCIANT ants of all."*

- ❑ Children play INSOUCIANTLY, as if they did not have a care in the world.

- ❑ Jake's INSOUCIANT behavior was inappropriate at his grandfather's funeral. It lacked respect for his memory.

- ❑ Her cheerful INSOUCIANCE was greatly admired by everyone in her office, but her husband says to wake up to such cheerfulness before he has had a cup of coffee is driving him up a wall.

SUNDRY
(SUN dree)
various, several, miscellaneous
Link: **SUNDAE**

*"Jimmy had SUNDRY ice cream
SUNDAES for his birthday."*

- ❏ A SUNDRY store is usually like a five and dime, a store carrying a variety of miscellaneous items for the household and personal use.

- ❏ SUNDRY articles in the newspaper written by parents and politicians would have you believe our school system leaves a lot to be desired.

- ❏ There were SUNDRY animals at the zoo.

CALLOUS
(KAL uss)
unfeeling, insensitive;
having calluses
Link: CALLUS

*"Jack was so CALLOUS, he called attention
to Mike's CALLUSES."*

❑ A CALLOUS remark about someone is a statement
that does not take into consideration the feelings
of another.

❑ It is hard to understand how CALLOUS some
people can be who ride in their limousines past
hoards of beggars in India and not pay them the
slightest attention.

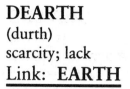

DEARTH
(durth)
scarcity; lack
Link: **EARTH**

*"There is a DEARTH of EARTH
in the middle of the ocean."*

❏ A DEARTH of rain last summer led to many failed crops, especially corn and cotton in the valley.

❏ This Broadway season was the poorest in years. Critics say this was largely due to a DEARTH of good playwrights.

❏ There always seems to be a DEARTH of cookies in the cookie jar after our granddaughter's visit.

REVERE
(ri VEER)
to regard with great devotion
or respect, to honor
Link: **PAUL REVERE**

*"Hero of the American Revolution,
PAUL REVERE is greatly REVERED."*

❑ Mother Teresa was greatly REVERED by all who knew of her humanitarian work in India.

❑ Another who enjoyed almost universal recognition and REVERENCE for his humanitarianism in the medical field was Dr. Schweitzer.

❑ Everyone REVERES Father Monahan; he is such a good and kindhearted pastor.

173

PROWESS
(PROW is)
exceptional skill and bravery
Link: **PROWLER**

"The PROWESS of a PROWLER."

- The PROWESS of the Sioux chief, Crazy Horse, in leading his warriors into battle, was legendary.

- Rod Laver's PROWESS as the world's best tennis player in the history of the game is supported by the fact that he won the Grand Slam twice. This has not been done since.

- Although Jody brags of his golf PROWESS, his friends say he is a meat-and-potato hacker.

GENERALIZE
(GIN er ul ize)
general rather than specific; to
form a general conclusion
Link: **GENERAL'S EYES**

*"To say that all GENERALS' EYES are
the same is to GENERALIZE."*

- ❑ Wilma's problem was she always GENERALIZED. Everything was either always bad or always good, and she could never specifically say what she liked or disliked.

- ❑ Our teacher asked us to be specific in our criticism and avoid GENERALIZATIONS.

- ❑ To say that all politicians are crooks and all lawyers are honest is to GENERALIZE. Broad GENERALIZATIONS are only partly true.

175

LEGACY

(LEG uh see)

something handed down from one who has
gone before or from the past; a bequest

Link: **LEG I SEE**

*"The LEG I SEE is my entire LEGACY from Great-
Grandfather Paul the Pirate."*

- ❑ The LEGACY of the copper mining industry is the
  creation of mountain wastelands where beautiful,
  unspoiled forests once stood.

- ❑ The fictional LEGACIES of the Old West in the
  late 1800s was of cowboys riding from town to
  town shooting at each other.

- ❑ The Johnson family's ancestral LEGACY was to
  have blonde hair and green eyes.

PHOBIA
(FOE bee ah)
a persistent, illogical fear
Link: **PHOTOS**

*"Some natives have a PHOBIA about PHOTOS,
believing their soul will be captured inside the box."*

❑ Those who have a PHOBIA about heights are said to be acrophobic.

❑ Claustrophobia is the PHOBIA of a person who fears small, confined spaces.

❑ Monophobia is the PHOBIA of being alone.

SOMBER

(SOM bur)

depressing, gloomy, dark

Link: SOME BEARS

"SOME BEARS endure winter hibernation in a SOMBER state of mind."

❑ You will find most everyone who attends a funeral wears SOMBER clothing, generally black or gray.

❑ He had the most SOMBER expression, and there was nothing we could to cheer him up, hardly what one might expect from a man getting married the next day.

❑ The music was anything but lively, and it soon cast a SOMBER spirit over the entire audience.

REVIEW #15: Match the word with its definition.

1. insouciant - (South Sea ant) a. carefree
2. sundry - (sundae) b. several, various
3. callous - (callus) c. scarcity of
4. dearth - (earth) d. handed down
5. revere - (Paul Revere) e. illogical fear
6. prowess - (prowler) f. insensitive
7. generalize - (generals' eyes) g. gloomy
8. legacy - (leg I see) h. skillful
9. phobia - (photos) i. to honor
10. somber - (some bears) j. general conclusion

Fill in the blanks with the appropriate word. The word form may need changing.

1. Although Jody brags of his golf _____, his friends say he is a meat-and-potato hacker.

2. Jimmy had _____ ice cream sundaes for his birthday.

3. South Sea ants are the most _____ ants of all.

4. A _____ of rain last summer led to many failed crops, especially corn and cotton in the valley.

5. Hero of the American Revolution, Paul Revere is greatly _____.

6. Those who have a _____ about heights are said to be acrophobic.

7. The _____ of the copper mining industry is the creation of mountain wastelands where beautiful, unspoiled forests once stood.

8. To say that all generals' eyes are the same is to _____.

9. A _____ remark about someone is a statement that does not take into consideration his/her feelings.

10. You will find most everyone who attends a funeral wears _____ clothing, generally black or gray.

179

EDIFICE
(ED uh fis)
a building, especially one of
imposing appearance or size
Link: **ATE A FACE**

*"The Great Kong ATE the north FACE of
the EDIFICE."*

- ❑ The construction of one EDIFICE led to another, and New York City became a skyline of enormous skyscrapers.

- ❑ The Taj Mahal may not be the largest EDIFICE ever constructed, but surely it is one of the most imposing in the world.

- ❑ Neither imposing in appearance or size, you could hardly refer to an outhouse as an EDIFICE.

PARADOX
(PAIR uh dahks)
a statement that seems true but at the same
time seems to also have an opposite truth
Link: **BEARS OR DUCKS**

"The 'are we BEARS or DUCKS' PARADOX."

- ❑ Dr. Jekyll was often a PARADOX; as soon as you began to understand him, he became Mr. Hyde.

- ❑ John said he was an agnostic, but the PARADOX was he attended church every Sunday.

- ❑ Herbert's hatred of walking was PARADOXICAL, once you understood he worked as a mailman.

PENITENT

(PEN uh tunt)

sorrow and remorse for past misdeeds

Link: **PENITENTIARY**

*"Bubba was PENITENT for the crimes that
landed him in the PENITENTIARY."*

- ❑ Clark became PENITENT when he learned his careless driving put two people in the hospital.

- ❑ The pickpocket pretended PENITENCE but the policeman believed him to be IMPENITENT.

- ❑ Jennifer felt PENITENT that she had cause her mother so much sorrow.

MUSE
(myooz)
to ponder; meditate;
think about at length
Link: FUSE

*"It is unwise to MUSE once
the FUSE is lit."*

- ❑ Rick was such a good auto mechanic he never MUSED over what the problem might be, he knew immediately and went right to work fixing it.

- ❑ Chess is a MUSING game of skill whereupon each player MUSES over all the possible moves before deciding which piece to move.

- ❑ Though the odds of winning the lottery are very low, it is fun to MUSE about what you would do if you actually won.

GLOAT
(gloat)
to brag greatly
Link: **GOAT**

"And I got this award for receiving so many awards," said the GLOATING GOAT.

- ❑ For years she GLOATED over the marriage of her daughter to the most eligible bachelor in town.

- ❑ If roosters can GLOAT, that rooster strutted all over the barnyard as if he were the proverbial cock of the walk.

- ❑ The mechanic said he didn't want to appear to GLOAT, but he did warn his customer last year he would have to fix it now or fix it later, and later would cost more.

PIQUE
(peek)
irritation, resentment stemming from
wounded pride; also to arouse curiosity
Link: **PEEK**

*"Jo Ann was PIQUED at her brother for
PEEKING at her slumber party."*

- ❑ The three sisters showed their PIQUE at not being invited to their cousin's wedding by their refusal to send wedding presents.

- ❑ Joey said he was PIQUED at the chemistry teacher for giving out final grades before he had time to finish his lab work.

- ❑ The sound of the car horn PIQUED our curiosity until we saw our neighbor had accidently pressed it while backing out of his driveway.

185

DISPEL
(dis PELL)
to drive away; to dissipate
Link: SPELL

*"The princess kissed many toads before she could
DISPEL the witch's SPELL on the prince."*

☐ After the crowd had been DISPELLED from the
scene of the accident, the wreckers hauled away
the tangled, wrecked automobiles.

☐ The professor told his student he wanted to
DISPEL any thoughts she might have of receiving
a better grade than she deserved just because he
was a good friend of the family.

RAMIFICATION
(ram uh fu KAY shun)
a branching out; a development growing out of
and often complicating a problem or pain
Link: **RAMS ON VACATION**

*"A possible RAMIFICATION of encountering
RAMS while ON VACATION."*

❑ Courtney did not realize being late for work three
mornings in a row would have RAMIFICATIONS
until her boss fired her.

❑ A RAMIFICATION is a development or consequence that grows from the main body as limbs
grow from trees and plants; therefore, there are
RAMIFICATIONS to every act a person makes no
matter how small, because every act has a consequence.

ALLURE
(uh LUHR)
to entice with something
desirable; tempt
Link: **LURE**

"Not all fish LURES ALLURE all fish."

- ❑ The ballet dancer's perfume was so ALLURING grown men fainted when she danced past.

- ❑ The sailors were ALLURED into believing that the calm, balmy seas would never become a ferocious storm.

- ❑ Psychologists find it puzzling, but all agree that movie stars have some indescribable ALLURING quality that movie audiences find irresistible.

COMMODIOUS
(kuh MOD dee us)
spacious, roomy, capacious
Link: COMMODE

"A COMMODIOUS COMMODE."

❑ The rooms in the castle were so COMMODIOUS that they were as large as the average home.

❑ In Hong Kong, the government has built several million apartments for the working class in recent decades. As compared to western standards, they are not very COMMODIOUS, only about half the size of a small, two-bedroom apartment in the United States.

189

REVIEW #16: Match the word with its definition.

1. edifice - (ate a face)
2. paradox – (bears or ducks)
3. penitent - (penitentiary)
4. muse - (fuse)
5. gloat - (goat)
6. pique - (peek)
7. dispel - (spell)
8. ramification - (rams on vacation)
9. allure - (lure)
10. commodious - (commode)

a. remorse for past deeds
b. ponder, meditate
c. a development
d. to entice, tempt
e. a building
f. to drive away
g. spacious
h. a brag
i. irritation
j. an opposite truth

Fill in the blanks with the appropriate word. The word form may need changing.

1. For years she _____ over the marriage of her daughter to the most eligible bachelor in town.

2. Courtney did not realize being late for work would have _____ until her boss fired her.

3. Not all fish lures _____ all fish.

4. The rooms in the castle were so _____ that they were as large as the average home.

5. John said he was an agnostic, but the _____ was he attended church every Sunday.

6. Clark became _____ when he learned his careless driving put two people in the hospital.

7. The Taj Mahal may not be the largest _____, but surely is one of the most imposing in the world.

8. The three sisters were _____ at not being invited to their cousin's wedding.

9. The princess kissed many toads before she could _____ the witch's spell on the prince.

10. Rick was such a good auto mechanic he never _____ over what the problem might be.

ORTHODOX
(OR thuh dahks)
conventional, doing it by the book,
sticking to established principles
Link: **THROW ROCKS**

*"In the times of the Roman Empire, it was
ORTHODOX to THROW ROCKS."*

- ❏ An ORTHODOX religion is one that holds fast to historical views that have not changed.

- ❏ The doctor's treatment for Judith's broken finger was ORTHODOX. He X-rayed the finger, set it in a splint, and told her to come back in a week.

- ❏ The ORTHODOX view of the earth is it is round. The views of those who still believe the world is flat, as many did in the thirteenth century, is UNORTHODOX.

FAWN

(fawn)

exhibit affection; seek favor through slave-like flattery; to "suck up" to something

Link: FAWN

"A FAWN FAWNING over his mother."

- ❑ The head of the movie studio didn't see through the FAWNING of all his underlings, believing they truly thought he was a genius.

- ❑ Mr. Johnson was a professional at "sucking up" to everybody he thought could help him advance in his career, a professional FAWNER from the word go.

- ❑ The grandmother FAWNED over her grandchild, tickling him and making goo-goo sounds.

LETHARGY
(LETH ur gee)
laziness, tiredness; languor
Link: **LEOPARD'S TEA**

"LETHARGIC LEOPARDS having TEA."

- ☐ There is nothing LETHARGIC about a cheetah chasing prey, as cheetahs are the fastest animals on earth.

- ☐ Cats are LETHARGIC because they have smaller hearts and lungs than other animals.

- ☐ His doctor told Jim he was in good health. His LETHARGY at work and at home was probably due to his being overweight, eating too much and exercising too little.

193

MASTICATE
(MAS tuh kayt)
to chew
Link: **MAST ATE**

LITTLE HENRY'S MASTICATING!!

POOR BABY'S TEETHING!

"Henry ATE the MAST when he started to MASTICATE."

- ❑ The doctor explained that a person's digestion is aided when they MASTICATE their food slowly.

- ❑ The Kiwi bird MASTICATES food before giving it to its young.

- ❑ The judge requested a recess to MASTICATE the facts presented by both the prosecution and the defense.

ARCHAIC
(ahr KAY ik)
belonging to an earlier time,
ancient; outdated
Link: CAKE

"An ARCHAIC CAKE."

- ❏ Her parents had an absolutely ARCHAIC idea of dating. She not only had to be in by nine o'clock, but her aunt chaperoned her on all her dates.

- ❏ ARCHAIC civilizations, those that aren't around anymore, are the chief subject of archaeological studies.

- ❏ Small countries that depend on agriculture for their economy will never raise their standard of living as long as they use ARCHAIC farm tools.

195

GAZEBO
(guh ZEE boe)
an outdoor structure with a
roof and open sides
Link: **ZEBRA**

"A ZEBRA GAZEBO on the Mari Mari Plains of Kenya, East Africa."

- ❑ A GAZEBO is most always found in a backyard or park.

- ❑ The GAZEBO in the mission courtyard was used for weddings in the summer. In the winter, goats would come and huddle together to stay warm and out of the rainy weather.

- ❑ On Sunday afternoons the family would gather together in the shade of our backyard GAZEBO.

196

ABHOR
(ab HOR)
to hate very much, to detest utterly
Link: CHORE

"The Booker boys ABHORRED doing CHORES."

❑ To ABHOR insects is to find them ABHORRENT.

❑ It is generally believed that most women have an ABHORRENCE of mice.

❑ It is a fact that most people ABHOR the thought of public speaking.

PLIGHT
(plyte)
a condition of situation, especially
a distressing one

Link: **FLIGHT**

"A PLIGHT in FLIGHT."

- ❑ In most dramatic stage plays, the PLIGHT of the good guys appears at its worse at the end of the second act.

- ❑ Determined to rescue the fifty hostages from their PLIGHT, the police rushed the aircraft before the terrorists could cause further harm.

- ❑ Christopher's friend advised him not to worsen the PLIGHT he had gotten himself into by starting a fight, which could only make matters worse.

CALLOW
(KAL oh)
immature and inexperienced
Link: **SHALLOW**

*"Our dad was so CALLOW he made his first
dive in our SHALLOW kiddie pool."*

❑ The CALLOW appearance of the troops he now
inspected reminded General Troister that wars kill
the youth of the nation, not the old politicians
who start them.

❑ The CALLOW boater did not have a life preserver
or a radio onboard his sailboat.

❑ CALLOW she was, but you never saw a more
enthusiastic, hard-working young lady at the glove
factory.

199

EUPHONIOUS
(you PHONE ee us)
pleasing to the ear
Link: **YOU PHONE US**

"You must be beautiful because you sound so EUPHONIOUS when YOU PHONE US."

❏ Carly sings in the choir because she has a sweet, EUPHONIOUS voice.

❏ The low, EUPHONIOUS croaking of the summer frogs was music to Jeff's ear.

❏ The grunting of a mature elephant seal is anything but EUPHONIOUS.

REVIEW #17: Match the word with its definition.

1. orthodox - (throw rocks) a. tiredness
2. fawn - (fawn) b. pleasing to the ear
3. lethargy - (leopard's tea) c. distressing situation
4. masticate - (mast ate) d. the established way
5. archaic - (cake) e. outdoor structure
6. gazebo - (zebra) f. an earlier time
7. abhor - (chore) g. inexperienced
8. plight - (flight) h. to chew
9. callow - (shallow) i. to detest
10. euphonious - (you phone us) j. exhibit affection

Fill in the blanks with the appropriate word. The word form may need changing.

1. It is a fact that most people _____ the thought of public speaking.

2. A _____ is almost always found in a backyard or park.

3. Carly sings in the choir because she has a sweet, _____ voice.

4. The doctor explained that a person's digestion is aided when they _____ their food slowly.

5. In the times of the Roman Empire, it was _____ to throw rocks.

6. _____ civilizations are the subject of archaeological studies.

7. The _____ boater did not have a life preserver or radio onboard his sailboat.

8. The head of the movie studio didn't see through the _____ of all his underlings.

9. In most dramatic stage plays, the _____ of the good guys appears at the end of the second act.

10. Cats are _____ because they have smaller hearts and lungs than other animals.

QUIRK
(kwurk)
a peculiarity of behavior; an
unaccountable act or event
Link: JERK

*"People have the strangest QUIRKS;
some can be real JERKS."*

❑ Watch out for this horse's QUIRK; he bucks every
time he sneezes.

❑ Have you ever noticed that Brad has the strangest
QUIRK? Every time someone mentions the word
"work," his leg jerks.

❑ It was a QUIRK of fate that Elizabeth was sick at
home the day her car pool had an accident.

MORES

(MAWR ayz)
customary cultural standards;
moral attitudes, manners, habits

Link: **MORE A's**

"Our educational MORES have it that the MORE A's a student makes, the better their education."

❑ According to Chinese MORES, it is considered polite for dinner guests to belch at the table as a gesture of appreciation and enjoyment.

❑ It is said that a certain actress of her acquaintance has dubious morals and disregards the accepted MORES for married women.

❑ The problem with some community MORES is that the older generation clings to outdated moral attitudes no longer appropriate for the times.

COMPRISE
(kum PRYZE)
to consist of; to include, to
contain, to be made up of
Link: **SURPRISE**

"It was not a pleasant SURPRISE when the pirates discovered their treasure was COMPRISED only of party favors."

- ❑ If we had one more kitten in the house, the litter would COMPRISE thirteen.

- ❑ A basketball team COMPRISES five players and any number of substitutes the coach wants to allow on the team.

- ❑ The first aid kit was COMPRISED of a bottle of aspirin, two gauze pads and a pair of scissors.

CACHE
(kash)
a hiding place, or the objects
hidden in a hiding place
Link: CASH

*"Escaped prisoner #5447 recovered the
CASH from his CACHE."*

❏ When Sam worked for the C.I.A., he directed a
movie on CACHING, how to hide booty where it
would not be discovered and would remain hidden
until an agent was ready to recover the contents.

❏ Treasure hunters have searched for Blackbeard's
treasure in Bahamian caves, but no one has yet
found his CACHE.

BUCOLIC

(byoo KAHL ik)
rural or rustic in nature,
country-like

Link: **BULLS FROLIC**

"BULLS FROLIC when a farm is BUCOLIC."

- ❏ The judges gave first prize to the painting of a BUCOLIC landscape in greens and blues.

- ❏ There is nothing BUCOLIC about big city life, honking horns and bustling streets are neither peaceful or rustic.

- ❏ Mr. Pride's farm with it's peaceful green pastures and a babbling brook, was the perfect BUCOLIC setting for a picnic.

AFFIDAVIT
(af uh DAY vit)
a sworn written statement
Link: **AFTER DAVID**

"AFTER DAVID slew Goliath, he made out an AFFIDAVIT not to further hurt any big guys."

- ❏ The defense lawyer had a sworn AFFIDAVIT from witnesses claiming his client was innocent of the crime charged against him.

- ❏ Roseanne had an AFFIDAVIT from her neighbor giving her permission to cut down the tree on their mutual property line.

- ❏ Too ill to appear before the county commission, the chairman accepted an AFFIDAVIT from the claimant.

ABSTRUSE

(ab STROOS)

hard to understand

Link: MOOSE

"His friends consider Mike, the MOOSE, to be very ABSTRUSE."

- ❑ Chemistry is an ABSTRUSE subject of study for many students.

- ❑ The scientists had many ABSTRUSE theories about atomic interactions.

- ❑ Elizabeth's directions to the party were very ABSTRUSE.

OBLIQUE
(oh BLEEK)
at an angle; indirect or evasive
Link: **FREAK**

*"Folks are not FREAKS just because
they walk OBLIQUELY."*

❑ To complement someone OBLIQUELY is to do so indirectly.

❑ The wall OBLIQUES from the entrance gate at a sharp angle (lines are said to be OBLIQUE if they are neither parallel or perpendicular to one another).

❑ The restaurant owner made OBLIQUE references to the impatience of his customers.

DILEMMA

(DEE lim ma)

a difficult situation where one must choose between two or more choices that seem unfavorable; any problem or predicament

Link: **LIMB**

"The DILEMMA facing Jake was to go over the waterfall or to grab the LIMB."

- ❏ John faced the DILEMMA of either taking a cut in pay or losing his job.

- ❏ Helen was on "the horns of a DILEMMA." She had to move with her family to another town and lose a semester in school or stay by herself until summer.

- ❏ It was a small DILEMMA, but Bill couldn't choose between pecan or cherry pie for dessert.

VERTIGO
(vur tuh GO)
the sensation of dizziness
Link: __WHERE TO GO__

"When test pilot Bob developed a bad case of
VERTIGO, he didn't know WHERE TO GO."

❑ Charles was acrophobic and even suffered from
VERTIGO while standing on a stool, replacing the
lights in the kitchen.

❑ A person said to have acrophobia is someone who
has a fear of great heights. Typically, acrophobes
suffer from VERTIGO if they are in a tall building
and look down.

REVIEW #18: Match the word with its definition.

1. quirk - (jerk)
2. mores - (more A's)
3. comprise - (surprise)
4. cache - (cash)
5. bucolic - (bulls frolic)
6. affidavit - (after David)
7. abstruse - (moose)
8. oblique - (freak)
9. dilemma – (limb)
10. vertigo - (where to go)

a. hard to understand
b. behavior peculiarity
c. cultural habits
d. sworn statement
e. dizziness
f. to be made up of
g. country-like
h. hiding place
i. at an angle
j. a difficult situation

Fill in the blanks with the appropriate word. The word form may need changing.

1. Treasure hunters have searched for Blackbeard's treasure, but no one has yet found his _____.

2. When test pilot Bob developed a bad case of _____, he didn't know where to go.

3. The _____ roof line makes it easy for rain water to run off.

4. Watch out for this horse's _____; he bucks every time he sneezes.

5. A basketball team _____ five players, and any number of substitutes.

6. The judges gave first prize to the painting of a _____ landscape in greens and blues.

7. Chemistry is an _____ subject for many students.

8. The defense lawyer has a sworn _____.

9. John faced the _____ of either taking a cut in pay or losing his job.

10. It is said that a certain actress of her acquaintance had dubious morals and disregards the accepted _____ for married women.

INTERVENE
(in tur VEEN)
to come between; to mediate,
to occur between times
Link: BETWEEN

"Referees INTERVENE BETWEEN player disputes."

☐ Harold and his twin brother might have argued all day if their father hadn't INTERVENED and said if they couldn't decide who would ride in the front seat, they could both sit in the back.

☐ So much had happened to the family in the INTERVENING years since Brett had gone off to college.

STUPEFY

(STOO puh fie)
to make numb with amazement;
to stun into helplessness

Link: **SUPER FLY**

*"The kids were STUPEFIED when SUPER FLY
stole the cake."*

❑ When Corporal Burch heard that an atomic bomb
   had been dropped on Japan and the war was over,
   he was STUPEFIED.

❑ The magician's trick left his audience STUPEFIED.

❑ The plumber seemed STUPEFIED when he could
   not fix the leaky faucet.

BLEAK
(bleak)
depressing, discouraging, harsh,
cold, barren, raw
Link: LEAK

*"Sometimes a simple LEAK can lead to
BLEAK consequences."*

- ❑ After Joy lost the first set six-love, the chances for the girl's tennis team to win the state championship began to look BLEAK.

- ❑ The vet said we should keep our hopes up, but the chance of our dog, Spot, surviving the car accident appeared BLEAK.

- ❑ The BLEAKNESS of the Aleutian Islands, where the winds howl constantly, makes one shiver just to see a picture of it.

AJAR
(uh JARR)
partially open

Link: **JAR**

"Hey, the JAR'S AJAR; we're outta here."

- ❑ When the police carefully examined the crime scene, they found a second-story window next to the large oak tree in the backyard had been left AJAR.

- ❑ Even though Mr. Kreamer had rejected the offer to sell his hardware store, he left the offer AJAR by saying he would reconsider after the Christmas season.

DEMUR
(dih MUR)
to object, to make exception
Link: **PURE**

"Cinderella was so PURE she DEMURRED from drinking even a root beer."

- ❑ Billy DEMURRED when his friends wanted him to run for class president.

- ❑ The mayor said he would DEMUR if asked to speak at the town rally.

- ❑ Nancy DEMURRED when Henry suggested she should share her lunch with he and his six friends.

CATHARSIS

(kuh THAR sis)

an emotional or psychological cleansing
that brings relief or renewal

Link: CATS AND HORSES

"CAT AND HORSE CATHARSIS."

- ❑ Psychologists now know that the companionship of domesticated pets can lead to a CATHARSIS for mentally disturbed patients.

- ❑ After Jeremy returned to the French World War II battlefield he had known fifty years before, he said he found the experience CATHARTIC.

ALLEVIATE
(uh LEE vee ayt)
to make less severe;
to relieve, to lessen
Link: **LEAVES ATE**

"The natives believed if they ATE the LEAVES of some trees, it would ALLEVIATE many illnesses."

❑ When Peter arrived with sacks of ice for the party, it ALLEVIATED the need to wait for the icemaker to produce more.

❑ When the team stopped for lunch, our coach ALLEVIATED the need for the waitress to bring separate checks when she offered to pay for all of us as a gesture of congratulations for our victory.

❑ Aspirin ALLEVIATES painful headaches most of the time.

219

DOMAIN
(DOUGH mane)
a territory over which one rules,
has influence or powers
Link: **PLAIN**

"Lions have DOMAIN over the PLAINS of Africa."

- ❑ When Minnesota Fats entered a pool hall, all the other players respectfully stopped their own games to watch, for they knew, this was his DOMAIN.

- ❑ The DOMAIN of the native Florida panther is in the Everglades and South Central Florida.

- ❑ The courtroom is the DOMAIN of attorneys and judges.

CANDOR

(CAN dur)

truthfulness, sincere honesty

Link: **CONDOR**

"A CONDOR with CANDOR."

- ❑ Speaking with CANDOR, the governor called for police reforms throughout the state.

- ❑ Without regard to feelings, our teacher said she would criticize our term papers with absolute CANDOR.

- ❑ The coach told his team that CANDOR means to speak honestly, and to speak CANDIDLY, the team stunk. (CANDID is showing CANDOR.

AFTERMATH

(AF tur math)

events following some occurrence;
a consequence of

Link: **AFTER MATH**

*"AFTER doing the MATH for calculating the atomic
bomb, Einstein would live to see the resulting
AFTERMATH.*

☐ Poverty and economic depression are usually the
  AFTERMATH of wars.

☐ An AFTERMATH of the bombing of Hiroshima
  was a modern new city that arose in its ruins.

☐ The AFTERMATH of Christina skipping classes
  too often to practice ballet was flunking Chemistry
  101.

REVIEW #19: Match the word with its definition.

1. intervene - (between)
2. stupefy - (super fly)
3. bleak - (leak)
4. ajar - (jar)
5. demur - (pure)
6. catharsis - (cats and horses)
7. alleviate - (leaves ate)
8. domain - (plain)
9. candor - (condor)
10. aftermath - (after math)

a. partly open
b. events following
c. to relieve, lessen
d. truthfulness
e. emotional relief
f. barren, depressing
g. ruling a territory
h. to object
i. come between
j. helpless amazement

Fill in the blanks with the appropriate word. The word form may need changing.

1. The burglars had entered the house from a second story window which had been left _____.

2. Referees _____ between player disputes.

3. Poverty and economic depression are usually the _____ of wars.

4. The mayor said he would _____ if asked to speak at the town rally.

5. The natives believed if they ate the leaves of some trees it would _____ many illnesses.

6. The _____ of the native Florida panther is the Everglades and South Central Florida.

7. When Corporal Burch heard that an atomic bomb had been dropped on Japan, he was _____.

8. The vet said our dog's chances of surviving the auto accident appeared _____.

9. Speaking with _____, the governor called for police reforms throughout the state.

10. Psychologists now know that the companionship of domesticated pets can lead to a _____ for mentally disturbed patients.

223

AFFINITY

(uh FIN uh tee)
a natural attraction;
kinship; similarity

Link: FIN TEA

*"The Chinese have an AFFINITY for shark
fin soup and shark FIN TEA."*

- ❑ Max had an AFFINITY for sports and excelled at football, basketball, and tennis.

- ❑ Monkeys have an AFFINITY for climbing, birds for flying and fish for swimming.

- ❑ A natural AFFINITY exists between monkeys and apes.

INVEIGLE

(in VAY gul)

to tempt or persuade by using
deception or flattery

Link: BAGEL

"The animal trainer INVEIGLED the lion to perform by tempting him with a BAGEL."

- ☐ My brother, Ryan, INVEIGLED me into doing his chemistry homework by promising to take my turn washing dishes for the next week.

- ☐ New York City street vendors INVEIGLE people into purchasing counterfeit Rolex watches for many times what they are worth.

DEMAGOGUE

(DEM uh gawg)

a leader who obtains power by appealing to the emotions and prejudices of the people

Link: **THEM DOGS**

"THEM DOGS, Hitler and Mussolini, were infamous DEMAGOGUES."

- ❑ Historians will almost exclusively agree that Hitler and Mussolini were DEMAGOGUES who were greatly responsible for starting World War II. (Demagogues are leaders, but not in a positive way.)

- ❑ Lawyers, politicians, and other authority figures who inflame the populace to further their own aims are said to be DEMAGOGUES who engage in DEMAGOGUERY.

BIZARRE

(bih ZAR)

extremely unconventional
or far-fetched

Link: **BAZAAR**

"You see some BIZARRE things for sale at a BAZAAR."

- ☐ It was a BIZARRE set of events that led to the violinist being in the small Swiss village, for it was here he met a young flutist who was to become his wife.

- ☐ As the medication began to take effect, Randolph's eyes took on a faraway look, and he muttered some BIZARRE nonsense about wanting to ride the pony one more time.

- ☐ "Wasn't he BIZARRE?" Lorna said of the strange man who appeared from nowhere and offered to give her an apple.

227

LAX
(lax)
careless, negligent; not tense, slack
Link: TAX

"This is what happens when you're
LAX in paying your TAX."

❑ When the bank security became LAX, it was then the bank robbers planned to rob the bank.

❑ Most bachelors are LAX in their housekeeping, but Mike and Bob set a record for LAXITY, as they only washed eating utensils when they were ready to eat.

❑ When they arrived at the dock, they found the ropes were LAX, and their boat was bumping against the dock.

CIRCA
(SUR ka)
about; at an estimated
historical time period
Link: **CIRCUS**

*"The first-known CIRCUS took place CIRCA
200,000 B.C."*

❑ The exact date of the first Egyptian dynasty is not
known, but it is believed to have occurred CIRCA
3000 B.C.

❑ CIRCA is another word for "about" or "more or
less," and always refers to a passage of time.

PIED
(pyed)
multi-colored, especially of more
than one color in patches
Link: **PIED PIPER**

"If you've ever wondered where the PIED PIPER got his name, it came from wearing PIED clothing."

❑ Hot-air balloons are most always PIED for safety purposes so they can be seen by powered aircraft that might be flying nearby.

❑ This season's hottest Paris fashion is PIED skirts.

❑ The PIED tuxedo James wore to the ball made him the subject of much attention.

HERBICIDE
(HERB uh side)
a substance used to destroy
plants, especially weeds
Link: **SUICIDE**

*"When weeds commit SUICIDE,
they use a HERBICIDE."*

❑ Environmentalists have proven that HERBICIDAL runoffs from farmland pollute our rivers, streams, and oceans.

❑ HERBICIDE is essential for controlling weeds in the production of fruits and vegetables.

❑ Ed completely destroyed his lawn after he mistook HERBICIDE for fertilizer.

MELANCHOLY

(MEL un kahl ee)

depression of spirits, gloomy, weary

Link: **MELON**

*"Farmer Brown was beset with MELANCHOLY
when he saw what the worms had done to his
MELON patch."*

❑ Sitting in her living room and thinking of her late husband brought a touch of MELANCHOLY to Aunt Mildred's remembrances of Uncle John.

❑ The best word to describe Jim is MELANCHOLY; no matter the situation, he always walks around looking like he had lost his best friends.

❑ It was a MELANCHOLY day, gloomy and dark.

(an TIR ee ur)
situated in front
Link: **ANTLERS**

"The ANTERIOR position of a deer's ANTLERS come in very handy."

- ❏ There is the ANTERIOR up front, the interior inside, the exterior outside, and the posterior bringing up the rear.

- ❏ The ANTERIOR of a stage is not as interesting as what takes place behind the scenes.

- ❏ The ANTERIOR of a ship is called the bow.

REVIEW #20: Match the word with its definition.

1. affinity - (fin tea)
2. inveigle - (bagel)
3. demagogue - (them dogs)
4. bizarre - (bazaar)
5. lax - (tax)
6. circa - (circus)
7. pied - (Pied Piper)
8. herbicide - (suicide)
9. melancholy - (melon)
10. anterior - (antlers)

a. evil leader
b. unconventional
c. natural attraction
d. persuade by deception
e. multi-colored
f. situated in front
g. estimated time period
h. depression of spirits
i. careless, negligent
j. plant poison

Fill in the blanks with the appropriate word. The word form may need changing.

1. It was a _____ day, gloomy and dark.

2. Historians agree that Hitler and Mussolini were _____ who started World War II.

3. Monkeys have an _____ for climbing, birds for flying and fish for swimming.

4. The animal trainer _____ the lion to perform by tempting him with a bagel.

5. _____ is another word for "about" or "more or less," and always refers to a passage of time.

6. When the bank security became _____, it was then the bank robbers planned to rob the bank.

7. The _____ of a ship is called the bow.

8. If you've ever wondered where the Pied Piper got his name, it came from wearing _____ clothing.

9. _____ is essential for the production of fruits and vegetables in controlling weeds.

10. It was a _____ set of events that led to the violinist being in the small Swiss village he never planned to visit.

234

EMBELLISH

(im BEL ish)
to beautify by adding ornaments; to
add fanciful or fictitious details to

Link: **BELLY**

*"BELLY dancers EMBELLISH their
BELLY buttons with jewels."*

❏ Every time Thomas caught fish, he would
EMBELLISH the size until you would think they
were as big as whales.

❏ A little EMBELLISHMENT to a story rarely hurts,
but makes the telling more engaging.

❏ Rod was eliminated as a job prospect when the
prospective employer learned he EMBELLISHED
his educational background to include a college
degree he did not possess.

PETULANT

(PET you lant)
ill humor, irritable, cranky

Link: **PET HUNT**

"The PET you gave me made me PETULANT."

- ❑ The PETULANT teacher slammed down her book and stalked angrily from the classroom. ·

- ❑ My mother told me not to play in the house the day my father lost his job, saying he was in a bad mood and very PETULANT.

- ❑ A PETULANT little creature, spoiled rotten by her parents, she had everything you could imagine and yet seldom ever smiled.

ASSUAGE
(uh SWAJE)
to soothe; to make less severe;
to satisfy, ease, lessen
Link: **MASSAGE**

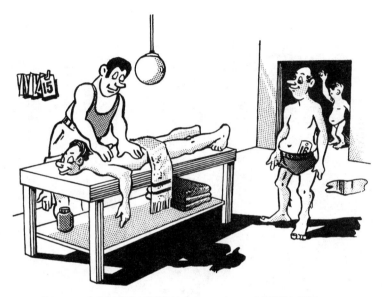

"A good MASSAGE is known to ASSUAGE sore muscles and relieve uptight feelings."

❑ When Jane double-faulted on match point, her coach came to her side and tried to ASSUAGE her disappointment by telling her she played a great tournament, but that no one is perfect.

❑ Dr. Moore was able to ASSUAGE the fear of his patient by predicting successful treatment.

❑ Many athletes drink Gatorade to ASSUAGE their thirst.

CASTIGATE
(KASS tuh gate)
to criticize harshly, usually with the
intention of correcting wrongdoing
Link: **PASSED THE GATE**

*"The gate attendant CASTIGATED Herman
for PASSING THE GATE."*

❑ The coach was CASTIGATED by the university's
administration for not recruiting football players
in compliance with NCAA regulations.

❑ Jimmy's mother CASTIGATED him for tracking
mud on their new living room carpet.

❑ When CASTIGATED for behavior unbecoming of
a naval officer, Chief Petty Officer Peterson was
denied shore-leave.

WREST
(rest)
pull away, take by violence
Link: **WRIST**

"The policeman grabbed the thief by the WRIST and WRESTED away his gun."

❑ Police will tell you that in dealing with a person who threatens you with a knife or a club, it is the best policy not to attempt to WREST the weapon away from them.

❑ When it was clear that the driver had too much to drink, the passengers WRESTED the keys away from him for their own safety.

PERVERSE

(pur VERS)

stubborn; contrary; intractable

Link: **REVERSE**

"Deadwood Dick's horse was so PERVERSE he often would go in REVERSE."

- ❏ Our neighbor Mike is a hateful person who takes a PERVERSE pleasure in having the worse kept lawn in the neighborhood.

- ❏ It is PERVERSE of Aunt Emma to make us wait for dinner when she can't eat steak with her false teeth anyway.

- ❏ The PERVERSENESS of the hunting guide was apparent; he had returned to camp without us and we were lost in the woods within the hour.

SERPENTINE
(sur pun TEEN)
snakelike in shape or movement;
winding as a snake
Link: **SERPENT TEEN**

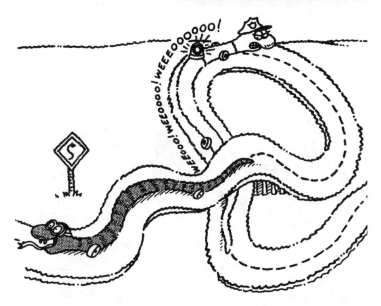

*"A SERPENT TEEN hot-rodding on a
SERPENTINE road."*

❑ Mountain roads SERPENTINE, winding around one mountain to the next.

❑ Really good mystery stories have SERPENTINE plots that lead the reader first one way, then back another, always keeping you guessing to the very end.

❑ Jack dashed through the line, SERPENTINING his way through tacklers until he scored the winning touchdown.

ABUT

(UH but)

border upon; to adjoin

Link: **BUTT**

"ABUTTING BUTTS."

- ❑ In Hong Kong the skyscrapers so closely ABUT each other, in some cases they touch sides.

- ❑ Texas ABUTS Mexico on its southern border.

- ❑ The ABUTTING rocks formed a perfect wall for riflemen to defend the castle.

SEGREGATE
(SEG rug gate)
to separate or keep apart
from others
Link: **SEPARATE GATE**

*"At the track, race horses are SEGREGATED into
SEPARATE GATES to begin the race."*

☐ The bulls were SEGREGATED into one pen and
the heifers SEGREGATED into another pen.

☐ To SEGREGATE truth from fiction is the duty
and obligation of every trial jury.

☐ The chairman asked the board to SEGREGATE
the facts from the rumors so they could arrive at a
reasonable course of action.

WITHER
(WITH ur)
shriveled, shrunken, dried-up
Link: WEATHER

*"Too much sun and too little rain makes corn
WITHER in the summer WEATHER."*

❑ A few WITHERED apples were all that remained
on the tree after the pickers had worked their way
through the orchard.

❑ He remembered her as a bouncy cheerleader. Fifty
years later he attended his high school reunion,
only to find she was still bouncy, but a bit
WITHERED with the passage of time.

REVIEW #21: Match the word with its definition.

1. embellish - (belly)
2. petulant - (pet)
3. assuage - (massage)
4. castigate - (passed the gate)
5. wrest - (wrist)
6. perverse - (reverse)
7. serpentine - (serpent teen)
8. abut - (butt)
9. segregate - (separate gate)
10. wither - (weather)

a. ill-humor
b. soothing
c. add ornaments
d. to adjoin
e. shrunken
f. stubborn
g. to separate
h. snake-like
i. criticize harshly
j. pull away

Fill in the blanks with the appropriate word. The word form may need changing.

1. Texas _____ Mexico on its southern border.

2. Too much sun and too little rain makes corn _____ in the summer weather.

3. Deadwood Dick's horse was so _____ he often would go in reverse.

4. The _____ teacher slammed down her book and stalked angrily from the classroom.

5. Every time Zachary caught fish, he would _____ the size until you'd think they were as big as whales.

6. Dr. Moore was able to _____ the fear of his patient by prescribing a successful treatment.

7. Mountain roads _____, winding around one mountain to the next.

8. At the track, race horses are _____ into separate gates to begin the race.

9. The gate attendant _____ Herman for passing the gate.

10. The policeman grabbed the thief by the wrist and _____ away his gun.

245

GRANDIOSE

(GRAN dee ohs)
grand and impressive, especially
flashy and showy

Link: **GRAND HOSE**

*"The GRANDIOSE Alaskan Pipeline resembles
nothing more than a GRAND HOSE."*

- ❑ Our coach had a GRANDIOSE plan to beat the
  Dallas Cowboys, only he didn't count on the fact
  they had a GRANDIOSE plan of their own.

- ❑ In all respects it was a simple enough house, unlike
  many others in that part of town. But the one
  exception was the GRANDIOSE fireplace in the
  family room, big enough to drive a truck through.

SURFEIT
(SUR fit)
an overabundant amount, especially
overindulgence in eating and drinking
Link: **SURFERS**

*"A SURFEIT of SURFERS is a sure path to
disastrous surfboard accidents."*

- ❑ Thanksgiving is a time when most families have large meals that are a SURFEIT for everyone at the table.

- ❑ The beach store had a SURFEIT of bathing suits and last Saturday put on a bathing suit sale.

- ❑ A SURFEIT of recruits showed up to try out for the team, and Coach Rex had to turn the freshmen away.

247

UNBRIDLED
(un BRIDE duld)
violent, unbounded, unrestrained
Link: **BRIDLE**

*"A wild horse without a BRIDLE can
be an UNBRIDLED demon to ride."*

- ❑ It is small wonder the children in that family are always in trouble; they are UNBRIDLED and do whatever they please.

- ❑ In last-minute desperation, the candidate made an UNBRIDLED speech full of deceitful accusations he hoped would discredit the mayor.

- ❑ Andrea's UNBRIDLED passion for dancing was evident in every performance she gave.

FORTUITOUS
(for TWO uh tus)
occurring by accident or chance

Link: FORTUNE FOR THE TWO OF US

*"FORTUITOUS FORTUNE FOR
THE TWO OF US."*

❑ Arriving at the opera at the last moment, it was FORTUITOUS there were seats available for the two of us.

❑ "The most FORTUITOUS event of my entire life," said President Roosevelt, "was meeting my wife, Eleanor."

❑ Missing the ill-fated flight because of the traffic jam on the way to the airport was FORTUITOUS to the extreme.

ENRAPTURE
(en RAP chur)
to delight, to thrill or give pleasure
Link: **CAPTURE**

*"The head-hunters were ENRAPTURED when they
CAPTURED Mr. and Mrs. Cranium."*

☐ John and Mary were ENRAPTURED when they
heard they had won a new car in the YMCA fund-
raising lottery.

☐ It was an ENRAPTURING performance. Everyone
was thrilled to attend the revival of Tennessee
Williams' play, *A Streetcar Named Desire*.

GUILE
(gyle)
craft, cunning, deceitfulness;
artfulness

Link: <u>MILE</u>

*Nobody could say Billy didn't use GUILE
when running the MILE."*

❏ Few people realized Bob's reputation as a shrewd businessman was due to his GUILE.

❏ The GUILE of the ticket scalper was shocking. He was selling tickets today for yesterday's matches.

❏ (BEGUILE is different from GUILE in that it is deception in a charming way.) Lois BEGUILED her beau with fetching flirtations.

MARSHAL

(MAHR shul)

to assemble together for the purpose of doing something; also an officer in the police or military

Link: **MARSHAL**

"The MARSHAL MARSHALED a posse to capture the Waco Kid."

❑ MARSHALING their forces, the British defeated Rommel at El Alamein.

❑ The Republicans MARSHALED their voters to firmly defeat the Democrats in the Congressional elections of 1994.

❑ The defense team MARSHALED its arguments before presenting them to the jury.

DESICCATE
(DES uh kayt)
to dry out completely;
dehydrate
Link: **THIS DRY CAKE**

*"Sharif, old buddy, THIS DRY CAKE has done
gone and got itself DESICCATED."*

- ❑ The drought was the worst in fifty years, and the olives on the trees were DESICCATED.

- ❑ The whale carcasses cast upon the beach had begun to DESICCATE by the time the marine biologist arrived at the scene.

- ❑ Raisins are grapes that have been shrunken and dried through a process of DESICCATION.

PHOTOGENIC
(phoh toe GIN ik)
suitable, especially attractive
for photography
Link: **PHOTO GENIE**

*"The PHOTOS of this PHOTOGENIC GENIE
could get her a television series."*

❑ Some movie actors and actresses are not all that
attractive in person, but have become successful
because they are very PHOTOGENIC on screen.

❑ Though not at all PHOTOGENIC, the Statue of
Liberty is probably the most photographed public
monument in the world.

RELINQUISH
(ri LING kwish)
to give up doing, professing, or
intending; to surrender, give in
Link: **REEL IN FISH**

*"Captain Ahab would never RELINQUISH
REELING IN the FISH."*

- ❑ I will never RELINQUISH my ambition to become a circus clown.

- ❑ Robert was a forty-year-old sore-arm, Class AA pitcher when he finally RELINQUISHED his dream of playing in the major leagues.

- ❑ The retiring C.E.O. merrily RELINQUISHED his control of the company with a wave from his yacht.

REVIEW #22: Match the word with its definition.

1. grandiose - (grand hose)
2. surfeit - (surfers)
3. unbridled - (bridle)
4. fortuitous - (fortune for two of us)
5. enrapture - (capture)
6. guile - (mile)
7. marshal - (marshal)
8. desiccate - (this dry cake)
9. photogenic - (photo genie)
10. relinquish - (reel in fish)

a. to be lucky
b. to dry out
c. overabundant
d. impressive, showy
e. unrestrained
f. cunning, crafty
g. to delight
h. take good photos
i. to surrender
j. assemble a group

Fill in the blanks with the appropriate word. The word form may need changing.

1. The marshal _____ a posse to capture the Waco Kid.

2. Our coach had a _____ plan to beat the Dallas Cowboys, but it back-fired.

3. The whale carcasses cast upon the beach had begun to _____ in the hot, summer sun.

4. John will never _____ his ambition to become a lawyer.

5. John and Mary were _____ when they had won a new car in the YMCA fund raising lottery.

6. It was _____ for the two of us that there were still seats available for the opera.

7. Her _____ passion for dancing was evident in every performance she gave.

8. The beach store had a _____ of bathing suits and last Saturday put on a bathing suit sale.

9. Because of their _____ qualities, actors are able to become successful movie stars..

10. Nobody could say Billy didn't use both speed and _____ when running the mile.

256

TYRO
(TY row)
a beginner; a novice
Link: **TIE ROPE**

"You could tell by the way Curly TIED ROPE,
that he was a cowboy TYRO."

- ❑ People never suspected that this was Henry's first marathon race; he ran the course like a veteran instead of a TYRO.

- ❑ What the forest rangers hated most was the 4th of July and other national holidays when hordes of camper TYROS invaded the park in their RV's and littered the forest, all of which had to be cleaned after they departed.

257

IDIOSYNCRASY
(id dee oh SINK ruh see)
a behavioral quirk; a person's idea about
behavior different from others
Link: **SINK CRAZY**

*"Waldo's artistic IDIOSYNCRASY is he's
SINK CRAZY."*

❑ Harriet had a way of smacking her lips every time
  you asked her a question, a harmless enough
  IDIOSYNCRASY, only it drove you crazy after a
  while.

❑ Jimmy Chen's habit of eating soup as a last course
  is no IDIOSYNCRASY; most Chinese have soup
  last instead of first as is the American custom.

ADJUNCT
(AJ unkt)
something connected or added to another
in a subordinate position; an assistant
Link: **ADD JUNK**

*"The tank driver ADDED JUNK as
an ADJUNCT to his tank."*

❏ Hang-gliding is only an ADJUNCT to Roseanna's
real love, which is skydiving.

❏ The library was an ADJUNCT to the Blakemores'
original home.

❏ The general's adjutant was not an ADJUNCT, but
a permanent part of his staff command.

YORE
(yore)
former days, an era long past
Link: **FLOOR**

*"In days of YORE, folks slept
on the FLOOR."*

❑ (YORE is generally to be seen in the phrase "days of YORE.") In days of YORE, my sister and I had to walk five miles to school in waist-deep snow.

❑ An exception to the word yore meaning a time long past would be the Royal House of YORE, which held the English throne from 1461 to 1485. But that of course, was in the days of YORE.

ABYSS
(uh BISS)
bottomless pit; a yawning gulf;
a profound depth or void
Link: MISS

*"The diver MISSED the ledge and sank
deep into the ABYSS."*

❑ The lost spaceship wandered endlessly in the vast ABYSS of the galaxy.

❑ After the rescuers dug without success for three days through the snow of the avalanche in search of the missing skier, they were disheartened and faced an emotional ABYSS of despair.

EMULATE

(IM u late)

to attempt to equal or surpass;
especially through imitation

Link: **IMITATE**

"Jimmy EMULATES his dad by IMITATING him."

- ❏ Most people EMULATE those they most admire.

- ❏ The famous golfer, Tiger Woods, has a golf swing that many golfers try to EMULATE.

- ❏ Pete EMULATED his older brother but was too small to make the baseball team.

ATYPICAL
(uh TIP uh cull)
not typical, abnormal
Link: **TYPICAL**

"Uncle Jeff's old bicycle is not TYPICAL of bikes today, it is ATYPICAL."

❑ A banana without a curve in it's length is ATYPICAL of the species.

❑ His parents agreed it was most ATYPICAL of John to stay home and study Saturday night when he could have gone to the movies with his friends.

CAJOLE
(kuh JOHL)
to wheedle, coax, or persuade someone
to do something they didn't want to
Link: **PAROLE**

*"Jimmy the Geek tried to CAJOLE the
warden into giving him a PAROLE."*

- ❑ Allison CAJOLED me into entering the marathon just so she could get a free T-shirt.

- ❑ Some of the younger Republicans were CAJOLED into voting for the Democratic candidate because he promised to lower the voting age.

- ❑ Jeannie always sweet-talked and CAJOLED her parents into letting her have her way.

BEREAVE
(buh REEV)
to be left alone, especially through
the death of another
Link: **LEAVE**

"BEREAVING the LEAVING of a friend."

❏ When their pony died, the BEREAVED children were told by their mother that everyone dies, and it was all right to cry and feel sad for a time.

❏ At his funeral procession, Jacqueline Kennedy's BEREAVEMENT over the death of her husband, President John F. Kennedy, was recorded on television for the entire nation to see.

❏ The BEREAVED widow wore a black dress to her husband's funeral.

265

LOITER
(LOY ter)
hang around; linger
Link: **LAWYER**

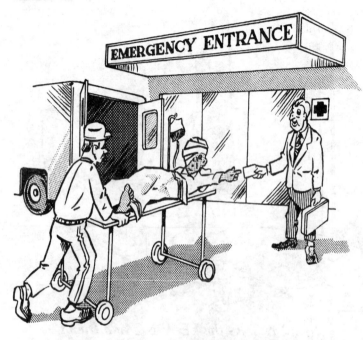

"Ambulance-chasing LAWYERS LOITER outside hospitals waiting for customers."

☐ A sign outside the players' entrance to the stadium said, "No LOITERING," but autograph hounds LOITERED there before and after games anyway.

☐ The supporting actor was on stage during most of the play, but he was so ineffective it was almost as if he were a LOITERER.

REVIEW #23: Match the word with its definition.

1. tyro - (tie rope)
2. idiosyncrasy - (sink crazy)
3. adjunct - (add junk)
4. yore - (floor)
5. abyss - (miss)
6. emulate - (imitate)
7. atypical - (typical)
8. cajole - (parole)
9. bereave - (leave)
10. loiter - (lawyer)

a. former days
b. something added
c. behavior quirk
d. to attempt to equal
e. to coax or persuade
f. abnormal
g. profound depth
h. a beginner
i. to hang around
j. suffering from the death of a loved one

Fill in the blanks with the appropriate word. The word form may need changing.

1. Jimmy the Geek tried to _____ the warden into giving him a parole.

2. Most people _____ those they most admire.

3. A shark without a dorsal fin is _____ of the species.

4. The _____ widow wore a black dress to her husband's funeral.

5. Ambulance-chasing lawyers _____ outside hospitals waiting for customers.

6. No one suspected this was Henry's first marathon race; he ran the course like a veteran instead of a _____.

7. The lost spaceship wandered endlessly in the vast _____ of the galaxy.

8. The library was an _____ to the Blakemores' original home.

9. In days of _____, my sister and I had to walk five miles to school in waist-deep snow.

10. Harriet had a way of smacking her lips, a harmless enough _____, only it drove you crazy.

LIEU

(loo)

instead of; in place of

Link: **BREW**

"In LIEU of a BREW, Billy The Kid had an orange soda."

❏ In LIEU of entering the university in September, Roger decided to work and save some money and start in January.

❏ Not wanting to lose her amateur standing after winning the U.S. Open singles title, Faye accepted the silver trophy in LIEU of the $545,000 first prize check.

EVOKE
(EE voke)
to summon forth, call to mind,
awaken, produce, suggest
Link: COKE

"Sometimes a song, a picture, even a COKE, can EVOKE the most poignant of youthful memories."

❑ A clap of thunder and a flash of lightning over the old castle EVOKED dark spirits for the villagers who remember the night of the headless ghosts.

❑ The demand made by the gymnastics coach for her gymnasts to give up dating and to spend weekends practicing EVOKED a strike by all the members of the team.

269

MAIM

(maim)

to disable or disfigure, to cripple

Link: **BLAME**

*"Roger MAIMED the bear's ear and
BLAMED Walter."*

❏ Joshua was a private in the U.S. Army and saw
action in the invasion of France where on the
sixteenth day after the landing, he was MAIMED
when he stepped on a land mine and lost his leg.

❏ Every year people are MAIMED in automobile
accidents by drunk drivers, the major cause of
highway accidents.

DEDUCE
(dee DOOS)
to come to a conclusion by reasoning
from the evidence
Link: MOOSE

"Marvin the MOOSE wondered why Elsie the cow couldn't DEDUCE that he was a MOOSE."

- ❑ When the doors to the living room were locked the day before Christmas, Peggy DEDUCED her mother was wrapping presents and didn't want to be disturbed.

- ❑ From the footprints in the snow, we DEDUCED that the missing hikers had wandered in circles several days before disappearing entirely.

- ❑ It is impossible for trial lawyers to DEDUCE what verdict a jury will bring in.

271

LEXICON
(LEX a ken)
a dictionary; vocabulary terms used in or
of a particular profession, subject or style

Link: **MEXICAN**

"A MEXICAN reading his LEXICON."

❑ The LEXICON used by air traffic controllers is
incomprehensible to non-pilots: "down wind to
twenty seven, hold three twenty at two thousand,
traffic at eleven o'clock, two miles."

❑ Sailors have a nautical LEXICON; "port means
left, starboard means right, bow means front and
stern means rear."

MENAGERIE
(muh NAJ uh ree)
a collection of live wild animals
on exhibit
Link: <u>LINGERIE</u>

"A MENAGERIE of LINGERIE."

- ❏ Busch Gardens has a wonderful MENAGERIE of lions, tigers, elephants and other wild animals roaming free and on display in a park-like setting.

- ❏ To have a house pet is one thing, but Susan keeps so many parrots and cats in her house, it is a virtual MENAGERIE.

- ❏ With twelve children in the family, the Jacksons referred to their offspring as their MENAGERIE.

PERMEATE
(PUR mee ayt)
to flow or spread through; penetrate
Link: **WORM HE ATE**

"The WORMS HE ATE PERMEATED the carcass."

- Corruption had PERMEATED every level of the government from the president to the dog catcher; they all belonged in jail.

- Before the explosion, witnesses said the smell of gasoline PERMEATED the flight cabin.

- Joshua was soaked clear through his raincoat; the rain had PERMEATED every inch of his clothing.

AMPLIFY
(AM pluh fi)
to make larger, louder, or
more powerful
Link: ANTS AND FLIES

*"Dr. Frankie AMPLIFIED the ANTS AND FLIES
to a monstrous proportion."*

❑ The music was AMPLIFIED to the point where the
guests couldn't hear themselves speak.

❑ General Rommel was unable to AMPLIFY the role
of his tank corps in the battle of El Alamein because he didn't have fuel to run them.

❑ Some actors attempt to AMPLIFY their roles by
upstaging their fellow actors.

275

CERTIFY
(SUR te fi)
to confirm formally; verify
Link: **HURT A FLY**

"George Washington never told a lie, and he would CERTIFY that he never HURT A FLY."

❏ The valuable papers arrived by CERTIFIED mail.

❏ In front of the entire commission, Jane was asked to CERTIFY she could prove her accusations.

❏ Jack was a CERTIFIABLE liar and crook, wanted in many countries by the authorities.

PARTITION
(PAR tish un)
the division of something into parts; an interior
structure dividing a larger area
Link: MAGICIAN

"The MAGICIAN creates a PARTITION."

- ❑ Korea was originally one country before being PARTITIONED into North and South Korea.

- ❑ Most college football teams are PARTITIONED into varsity and "scrubs," the "scrubs" being those trying to make the varsity team.

- ❑ In most tennis clubs there are fence PARTITIONS separating the courts from each other.

REVIEW #24: Match the word with its definition.

1. lieu - (brew)
2. evoke - (coke)
3. maim - (blame)
4. deduce - (moose)
5. lexicon - (Mexican)
6. menagerie - (lingerie)
7. permeate - (worm he ate)
8. amplify- (ants and flies)
9. certify - (hurt a fly)
10. partition - (magician)

a. to confirm
b. in place of
c. call to mind
d. special dictionary
e. to disable
f. to divide
g. flow through
h. animal collection
i. come to a conclusion
j. make larger

Fill in the blanks with the appropriate word. The word form may need changing.

1. In front of the entire commission, Jane was asked to _____ that she could prove her accusations.

2. The _____ used by air traffic controllers is incomprehensible to non-pilots.

3. In _____ of entering the university in September, Roger decided to work and enter the next term.

4. The music was _____ to the point where the guests couldn't hear themselves speak.

5. Before the explosion, witnesses said the smell of gasoline _____ the flight cabin.

6. In most tennis clubs there are fence _____ separating the courts from each other.

7. Every year people are _____ in automobile accidents by drunk drivers.

8. Sometimes a song, a picture, even a coke, can _____ the most poignant of youthful memories.

9. It is impossible for trial lawyers to _____ what verdict a jury will bring in.

10. To have a pet is one thing, but Susan has so many parrots and cats at home, it's a virtual _____.

278

JOUST

(joust)

a combat with lances between two knights, a tilting match; any combat suggestive of a joust

Link: **MOUSE**

"A JOUSTING MOUSE in King Arthur's time."

- ❑ Running and enjoying the competition, Bill and Harry JOUSTED each other playfully.

- ❑ It was a JOUSTING match to the death between Sir Lancelot and the Black Knight.

- ❑ Her toes all bruised, Sue Ellen declared it wasn't a dance, but a JOUSTING match.

INFAMY

(in fa MEE)

having an evil reputation;
extreme disgrace

Link: **FAMILY**

*"Blackbeard the Pirate's FAMILY will
live in INFAMY."*

❑ Western outlaws such as Jesse and Frank James
have been made heroes in movies, but in reality
they were INFAMOUS for their bad deeds.

❑ The INFAMIES of Germany's Adolf Hitler will
live for eternity.

❑ The great white shark has been made INFAMOUS
by the movie *Jaws*.

NEPOTISM

(NEP uh tiz um)
favors shown by those in high
positions to relatives and friends

Link: **NEPHEWISM**

"Mr. Roberts, the C.E.O. of the company, shows a little NEPOTISM toward his NEPHEW."

❑ Totally inept, Howard was a real estate agent for the company only because his uncle, the president, was not above a little NEPOTISM.

❑ NEPOTISM is an acceptable way of life in Central American countries.

FLEECE

(fleece)

to defraud, swindle; also the wool
of a sheep or similar animal

Link: **FLEEING**

"FLEEING with the FLEECE."

- ❑ It was spring on the Australian sheep farms, the time of year when the sheep are FLEECED for their wool.

- ❑ The housewives on our street were FLEECED by a con man selling bogus magazine subscriptions.

- ❑ Jim had larceny in his heart all his life and would sooner FLEECE a customer than make an honest deal.

PARRY

(pary)

to ward off a blow; to turn aside;
to avoid skillfully, to evade

Link: **PEAR**

"The PEARS PARRIED each other's fencing movements."

- ❏ The boxers PARRIED blows as each waited for an opening to strike a knockout punch.

- ❏ PARRYING with respective verbal arguments, the politicians blamed each other for the increase in statewide crime.

- ❏ The knights charged Robin Hood's men, who PARRIED their lances with limbs from the trees in Sherwood Forest.

PERIPHERY

(puh RIF uh ree)
the outermost part within a
boundary, the outside edge

Link: **REFEREE**

*"REFEREES would be wise to stay outside
the PERIPHERY of a boxer's reach."*

- ❑ On the PERIPHERY of any argument, Jasmine will
  listen but rarely ever speak.

- ❑ Colonel Mason posted guards at the PERIPHERY
  of the camp for night security.

- ❑ What you see out of the corner of your eyes is your
  PERIPHERAL vision (looking straight ahead and
  seeing to the side).

ENTOMOLOGY
(IN toe mol o gee)
the scientific study of insects
Link: **APOLOGY**

*"An ENTOMOLOGIST making his APOLOGY
to the insects he must study."*

- ❑ The primary function of ENTOMOLOGISTS is to discover how to prevent insects from destroying crops.

- ❑ (Many words ending in GIST refer to a person of science in their particular field.) A GEOLOGIST studies the earth; a PSYCHOLOGIST is a scientist of human behavior; and a METEOROLOGIST is a person who studies the atmosphere and weather.

OSTRACIZE
(AHS truh syze)
to exclude from a group;
to shun
Link: OSTRICH

*"Ozzie the OSTRICH wondered why he was being
OSTRACIZED from the group."*

❑ Andre felt OSTRACIZED by the members of the
club, but the truth was they couldn't understand
his accent.

❑ After gaining a reputation as a cheap-shot player
with the Pittsburgh Steelers, he joined the Dallas
Cowboys only to find he was OSTRACIZED by
the Dallas players as well.

CAPACIOUS
(kuh PAY shush)
roomy, able to hold much
Link: **CAP SPACIOUS**

"A SPACIOUS CAP is CAPACIOUS."

☐ The old castle has a CAPACIOUS dining room large enough to seat a small army.

☐ David's memory for jokes is CAPACIOUS; he remembers them all.

☐ Our bed at the hotel was really CAPACIOUS; all three sisters slept there.

FICKLE
(FIK ul)
often changing for no reason;
not loyal or consistent
Link: **PICKLE**

*"Pregnant women are very FICKLE; one moment
they want ice cream, the next, PICKLES."*

❑ The summer weather is always very FICKLE, each
morning the sun shines, but when you are ready to
play golf, it starts to rain.

❑ The FICKLE girl is one whose boyfriend is the one
she is holding hands with at the moment.

❑ Coach Adams' FICKLENESS was known by all his
players; he would say you were the best player on
the team, but would replace you the first time you
made a mistake.

REVIEW #25: Match the word with its definition.

1. joust - (mouse)	a. favors to relatives
2. infamy - (family)	b. to avoid a blow
3. nepotism - (nephewism)	c. to swindle
4. fleece - (fleeing)	d. a tilting match
5. parry - (pear)	e. to be excluded
6. periphery - (referee)	f. changeable
7. entomology - (apology)	g. bad reputation
8. ostracize - (ostrich)	h. roomy
9. capacious - (cap spacious)	i. study of insects
10. fickle - (pickle)	j. the outside edge

Fill in the blanks with the appropriate word. The word form may need changing.

1. The _____ of Germany's Adolf Hitler will live for eternity.

2. The science of _____ is the study of insects.

3. Our bed at the hotel was really _____, all three sisters slept there.

4. Pregnant women are very _____; one moment they want ice cream, the next, pickles.

5. The housewives on our street were _____ by a con-man selling bogus magazine subscriptions.

6. _____ is an acceptable way of life in Central American countries.

7. Running and enjoying the competition, Bill and Harry _____ each other playfully.

8. The boxers _____ blows as each waited for an opening to strike a knockout punch.

9. Colonel Mason posted guards at the _____ of the camp for night security.

10. Andre felt _____ by the members of the club, but the truth was they couldn't understand his accent.

MARAUDER

(muh RAWD er)

raider, intruder

Link: **MA RAIDER**

"The fiercest MARAUDERS are MA RAIDERS."

❑ Among the legendary pirate MARAUDERS of the eighteenth century were Captain Kidd, Calico Jack Rackam, Charles Vane, Blackbeard and Sir Henry Morgan.

❑ Christine referred to her husband Christopher as a kitchen MARAUDER for his midnight raids on the ice box.

❑ During the Civil War, MARAUDING bands of Confederate guerrillas raided Union supply lines in the Midwest.

EMIT
(EE mit)
to send or give out; to express, utter;
to put in circulation as money
Link: SPIT

*"Uncle Otto sure could EMIT a
lot of chewing tobacco SPIT."*

- ❑ The new federal laws on automobile EMISSIONS are directed at reducing pollution on our nation's highways.

- ❑ The mayor spoke on crime, EMITTING the most nonsense I have ever heard on that subject.

- ❑ David told the mechanic that the car EMITTED a strange sound when he started the engine.

ENGULF

(in GULF)

to surround or enclose completely

Link: **GULF**

*"The GULF of Mexico ENGULFS
many deserted islands."*

- ❑ The movie stars were ENGULFED by a swarm of paparazzi as they arrived at the Academy Awards ceremony.

- ❑ An ENGULFING movement by the Union troops cut off the Confederate retreat.

- ❑ The hurricane completely ENGULFED the town in a surge of wind and water.

UMBRAGE
(UM bridge)
sense of injury or insult; to take
offense, displeasure
Link: DUMB BRIDGE

*"Mike, the engineer, took UMBRAGE when
people called it a DUMB BRIDGE."*

❑ Polly took UMBRAGE when her husband told her
she was wearing too much makeup and looked
older than she was by trying to look younger than
she was.

❑ "I take UMBRAGE at your remarks about my golf
game," Theodore said jokingly to his regular golf
partner. "I'm the only one you can beat."

ABOMINATE
(uh bahm uh NAYT)
extreme hatred, loathing;
something despised
Link: A BOMB HATE

"I ABOMINATE BOMBS."

- ❑ The movie was a total ABOMINATION of good taste, containing needless violence from the beginning to the end.

- ❑ Jackie shuddered with ABOMINATION at the thought of eating wild pig for dinner.

- ❑ Cousin Rachel ABOMINATED her relatives when they came to visit her and tracked mud on her new white carpet.

RIVET

(RIV it)
something that fastens two parts together;
also to hold the attention of
Link: **RIVET**

*"The audience was RIVETED to their
seats watching the RIVETER."*

- ❏ Some actors have a certain charisma; once they appear on stage all eyes are RIVETED upon them.

- ❏ Most naval ships, army tanks and fighter aircraft have metal plates for their outer bodies that are held together by RIVETS.

- ❏ The kids are always RIVETED to the television on Saturday mornings.

RUDIMENTARY
(roo duh MEN tuh ree)
basic, crude, undeveloped; fundamental
principles or skills
Link: **RUDE ELEMENTARY**

*"RUDE children in ELEMENTARY school are often
RUDIMENTARY by nature."*

- ❑ "RUDIMENTARY, my dear Watson," Sherlock Holmes used to say to Dr. Watson when he had uncovered an important clue to a murder.

- ❑ If Tarzan lived with apes all his life, his social skills must have been very RUDIMENTARY.

- ❑ The eating utensils and tools of early cave dwellers during the Ice Age were very RUDIMENTARY.

ABRIDGE

(uh BRIJ)
to shorten; to condense;
to diminish; to curtail

Link: **BRIDGE**

"An ABRIDGED BRIDGE."

- ❑ If you don't want to read an entire newspaper to learn the latest daily news, there are clipping services that will ABRIDGE news stories to your specifications.

- ❑ An ABRIDGED dictionary or thesaurus is one that has been shortened.

- ❑ We saw an ABRIDGEMENT of the movie *Gone With the Wind* on TV last night; it only lasted two hours whereas the original lasted four.

FESTER

(festur)

to generate pus; to become a source
of resentment or irritation

Link: **UNCLE FESTER**

*"UNCLE FESTER likes to pick his scabs
and watch them FESTER."*

- ❏ Diane's FESTERING resentments toward her boss finally drove her to quit her job.

- ❏ Private Sholley's wounds had FESTERED for so long it was nearly impossible for the surgeons to save his leg.

- ❏ Coach Jones' resentments toward the complaining players on the team FESTERED until he finally told them to shut up or quit.

ENTOMB

(in toom)
to place in or as if in a tomb,
or a grave

Link: ROOM

*"Ahmed, you fool, you have ENTOMBED
us in the burial ROOM."*

- ❏ The Egyptians ENTOMBED their kings in special burial chambers together with all their possessions needed in the afterlife.

- ❏ There have been cases where people, thought dead, were ENTOMBED while still alive.

- ❏ In the Pittsburgh coal mine disaster of 1938, thirty-six coal miners were ENTOMBED in a tunnel for thirteen days. Only fourteen survived.

REVIEW #26: Match the word with its definition.

1. marauder - (ma raider)
2. emit - (spit)
3. engulf - (gulf)
4. umbrage - (dumb bridge)
5. abominate - (a bomb hate)
6. rivet - (rivet)
7. rudimentary - (rude elementary)
8. abridge - (bridge)
9. fester - (Uncle Fester)
10. entomb- (room)

a. surround
b. hold attention
c. to place in or bury
d. undeveloped, basic
e. something despised
f. source of irritation
g. to condense, shorten
h. intruder; raider
i. take offense
j. to give out

Fill in the blanks with the appropriate word. The word form may need changing.

1. The eating utensils and tools of early cave dwellers during the Ice Age were very _____.

2. During the Civil War, _____ bands of Confederate guerrillas raided Union supply lines.

3. Polly took _____ when her husband told her she was wearing too much makeup.

4. Jackie shuddered with _____ at the thought of eating wild pig for dinner.

5. The audience was _____ to their seats watching the riveter at work.

6. Uncle Otto sure could _____ a lot of chewing tobacco spit.

7. The hurricane completely _____ the town in a surge of wind and water.

8. An _____ dictionary or thesaurus is one that has been shortened.

9. Egyptian kings were _____ in special burial rooms.

10. Private Sholley's wounds had _____ for so long it was nearly impossible for the surgeons to save his leg.

300

EXHUME
(EKS hume)
to dig up from a grave; to bring to
light, uncover
Link: TOMB

"Archeologists like to EXHUME TOMBS."

❑ The judge issued a court order to EXHUME the grave of an unknown soldier.

❑ Historians EXHUMED the literary reputation of novelist Jack London.

❑ Mrs. Brown EXHUMED old love letters sent to her by her husband before they were married.

LAUDABLE
(LAWD uh bul)
worthy or deserving of praise
Link: **APPLAUDABLE**

*"A LAUDABLE performance that
was APPLAUDABLE."*

- ❑ Hector's teacher told him she thought it most LAUDABLE that he wanted to become a doctor, but an F in biology was not going to help him achieve his goal.

- ❑ During the rainy season it appeared LAUDABLE of Tim to bring an umbrella and escort the girls to their bus after school. That is, until they found out he was running for student president.

ALTERCATION
(awl tur KAY shun)
to argue vehemently,
a heated quarrel
Link: **ALTAR**

"An ALTERCATION at the wedding ALTAR."

❑ The Mafia had a slight ALTERCATION with the police, and ten Mafiosa were arrested and booked in downtown Manhattan.

❑ The Sioux Indians were not looking for an ALTERCATION, but when General Custer's men attacked their village, the Sioux wiped out Custer and his troops in self-defense.

❑ When Professor Pit said it was the South who had started the Civil War, an ALTERCATION broke out among the students.

DECREE
(dih KREE)
an order having the force of law
Link: **SET FREE**

*"The governor DECREED that all the
prisoners be SET FREE."*

❑ The DECREE by the city council that all dogs must
be kept on a leash set off a bitter conflict among
dog owners.

❑ In Dodge City, during the days of the great cattle
drives of the 1880s, Sheriff Wyatt Earp enforced
the DECREE that all guns must be turned over to
the sheriff's deputies before a man could ride into
town.

GAMIN
(GAM in)
a neglected boy left to run about
in the streets
Link: JAMMIN'

"A JAMMIN' GAMIN."

❑ In India, everywhere our tour bus stopped, there would be a gang of GAMINS begging for money, but if you dared give a rupee to one, a hundred more would immediately appear.

❑ In the novel, *Oliver Twist*, we learn of the intolerable living conditions in English orphanages of the nineteenth century and the life of the many home-less, streetwise GAMINS.

DEBASE

(di BAYS)
lower in quality,
character or value

Link: **THE BASE**

"Big Bertha easily DEBASED THE BASE."

- ❑ The inflation in Brazil has so DEBASED the value of money that people won't stoop to recover small coins in the street.

- ❑ The judge sued the newspaper for DEBASING his character in an article claiming he was too easy on criminals.

- ❑ Violent crime in America DEBASES our country.

DAUNTLESS
(dawnt liss)
to be fearless; unintimidated
Link: **HAUNTLESS**

*"The DAUNTLESS ghostbusters render a
haunted house HAUNTLESS."*

- ❑ DAUNTLESS and determined, the firemen dashed through the smoke to rescue the family trapped in the fire. UNDAUNTED by the flames, they stayed until everyone had been rescued. (DAUNTLESS and UNDAUNTED mean the same thing.)

- ❑ The hikers were UNDAUNTED by the steepness of the mountain; however, they decided to turn back for the sake of their own safety.

CHIDE
(chide)
scold; reprove
Link: **LIED**

*"The good fairy CHIDED Pinocchio
because he LIED."*

❏ When Bobby threw his toys against the wall, his
father CHIDED him for his bad temper.

❏ I don't mind being CHIDED for things I did, but
I hate being CHIDED for what my sneaky sister
Elizabeth did.

❏ The sergeant told the private that he was going to
CHIDE him each time he didn't properly clean his
rifle.

SPURN
(spurn)
to reject with disdain
Link: BURN

"Robert was BURNED when Rebecca
SPURNED him."

❑ James talked of nothing but how much he wanted a date with Ruth, but would never ask her for fear she would SPURN him.

❑ John thought he made a fair offer for the house, but the owner SPURNED his offer and actually became angry about it.

❑ When Jimmy Connors won the tennis match and offered to shake hands with his opponent, the loser SPURNED Jimmy's hand and walked off.

FEIGN

(fayn)

to give a false appearance;
to pretend

Link: **INSANE**

*"The prisoner FEIGNED INSANITY
as a defense to his crime."*

☐ Jeremy talked a good game but FEIGNED knowledge of space science he did not possess.

☐ Elizabeth FEIGNED illness in order to stay home from school the day of her final exam in math.

☐ (Any FEIGNED action is a FEINT.) The boxer kept FEINTING with his left hand, waiting for an opening to hit a knockout punch with his right.

REVIEW #27: Match the word with its definition.

1. exhume – (tomb)
2. laudable - (applaudable)
3. altercation - (altar)
4. decree - (set free)
5. gamin - (jammin')
6. debase - (the base)
7. dauntless - (hauntless)
8. chide - (lied)
9. spurn - (burn)
10. feign - (insane)

a. scold
b. to lower in quality
c. order by law
d. to pretend
e. street kid
f. to reject
g. to dig up
h. heated quarrel
i. fearless
j. worthy of praise

Fill in the blanks with the appropriate word. The word form may need changing.

1. The prisoner _____ insanity as a defense to his crime.

2. During the rainy season it was _____ of Tim to bring an umbrella and escort the girls to class.

3. Archeologists like to _____ tombs.

4. The inflation in Brazil has so _____ the value of money that people won't pick coins off the street.

5. James never asked Ruth out on a date for fear she would _____ him.

6. _____ and determined, the firemen dashed through the smoke to rescue the family.

7. The Mafia had a slight _____ with the police after ten of their members were arrested.

8. In India, everywhere our tour bus stopped, there would be a gang of _____ begging for money.

9. The good fairy _____ Pinocchio because he lied.

10. The _____ by the city council that all dogs must be kept on a leash set off a bitter conflict among dog owners.

311

DAMPER
(DAM per)
one that depresses
or restrains
Link: **DAMP PAW**

"A DAMP PAW can put a DAMPER on a good time."

- ❏ The jury trial seemed to be going the way of the defense until an eyewitness put a DAMPER on the defendant's hopes by identifying him as the one who committed the crime.

- ❏ The family was excited about their vacation until their father put a DAMPER on their plans, saying he was sorry, but there was no money for a vacation this year.

SCAPEGOAT
(SCAPE goat)
one who is made an object
of blame for others
Link: **GOAT**

*"I ask you, does this man look
like a SCAPEGOAT?"*

- ❑ Mary said she was not one of the sorority sisters who stayed out late, and she wasn't going to be the SCAPEGOAT for the ones who did.

- ❑ Henry was always the SCAPEGOAT, taking blame for whatever happened, whether he was to blame or not.

HUSBANDRY
(HUZ bun dree)
management of resources, especially
in agriculture
Link: **HUSBAND TREE**

*"To help in her HUSBANDRY chores, Aunt
Emma had her own HUSBAND TREE."*

- ❑ (HUSBANDRY is the practice of conserving resources; to HUSBAND is to economize.) Experts say the world's oil resources will soon be exhausted, and we must soon begin to HUSBAND oil.

- ❑ Everyone in our squad HUSBANDED their share of water for the long trek back to the barracks.

SPUR
(spur)
to move to action; an incentive
Link: SPURS

*"SPURS are called SPURS because
they SPUR a horse to action."*

☐ The coach told his players that his job was not
only to teach, but to SPUR them on to do their
best.

☐ The general SPURRED his troops to make one last
effort to take the hill.

☐ The principal's talk on good citizenship SPURRED
the students into not littering the school grounds.

TRUCULENT

(TRUK yu lunt)
inclined toward conflict;
eager to fight
Link: **TRUCK YOU LENT**

*"The TRUCK YOU LENT Uncle Frank
made him TRUCULENT."*

- ❑ Looking back on it, we never understood what made Randolph TRUCULENT all through school; he always had a chip on his shoulder.

- ❑ A TRUCULENT attitude seldom wins friends or influences people in a positive way.

- ❑ Just because your birthday cake was full of bugs, you don't have to be so TRUCULENT about it.

DEBACLE
(di BAHK ul)
a sudden calamitous downfall;
collapse or failure
Link: **THE BUCKLE**

*"When THE BUCKLE broke, Shakespeare's
Hamlet became a DEBACLE."*

- ❏ It was an absolute DEBACLE for Agassi as he lost the third set without winning a single point.

- ❏ The bank went broke as a result of a DEBACLE created by the thieving board of directors.

- ❏ A worse DEBACLE you would never hope to see; it rained on the Easter parade.

OPTIMUM
(OP tuh mum)
the most advantageous; the best
condition, degree, or amount
Link: OCTOPUS MOM

*"An OCTOPUS MOM has the OPTIMUM
ability to feed her young."*

- ❏ Fran said she had the OPTIMUM job, working at home on the word processor while watching soap operas.

- ❏ As the conditions were OPTIMUM, with no wind at the track, the U.S. Olympic team had hopes of breaking the world record in the 440 yard relay.

- ❏ With Rudy unemployed, his wife in the hospital, and the three children sick with the flu, this was hardly an OPTIMUM situation for the family.

COUTURE
(KOO chur)
fashion and fashion designers
Link: **FUTURE**

*"That's what we'll be wearing, the COUTURE
of the FUTURE."*

❑ Jane works for a department store chain and they sent her to Paris to study the latest COUTURE.

❑ Henry studied the art of COUTURIER for three years in the finest French design institutions.

❑ COUTURE, pewture, I'll wear what I please and those Frenchie guys can go fiddle-faddle all they want.

SUPPLANT
(suh PLANT)
to take the place of
Link: **PLANT**

*"Gardeners PLANT new plants to
SUPPLANT old PLANTS."*

- ❑ After the school superintendent retired, she was SUPPLANTED by the deputy superintendent.

- ❑ The Recreation and Parks Department's proposed budget for next year was quickly SUPPLANTED by a budget mandated by the Board of County Commissioners.

- ❑ The scheduled boxing match was postponed and SUPPLANTED with a Hawaiian dance contest.

QUANDARY

(KWAHN dree)

state of perplexity; difficult or
uncertain situation

Link: **LAUNDRY**

"A QUANDARY in the LAUNDRY."

- ❑ The police were in a QUANDARY; the butler's fingerprints were all over the murder weapon, but he was two thousand miles away and appearing on the *Tonight Show* during the time the murder was committed.

- ❑ When a girl likes two boys equally well and they each ask her for a date at the same time, that is a teenage QUANDARY of major proportions.

REVIEW #28: Match the word with its definition.

1. damper - (damp paw)
2. scapegoat - (goat)
3. husbandry - (husband tree)
4. spur - (spurs)
5. truculent - (truck you lent)
6. debacle - (the buckle)
7. optimum - (octopus mom)
8. couture - (future)
9. supplant - (plant)
10. quandary - (laundry)

a. manage resources
b. uncertain situation
c. take the place of
d. act of depression
e. move to action
f. eager to fight
g. fashion
h. collapse, failure
i. most advantageous
j. object of blame

Fill in the blanks with the appropriate word. The word form may need changing.

1. Mary said she wasn't the one who stayed out late, and that she wouldn't be the _____ for those who did.

2. Just because your birthday cake is full of weevils, you don't have to be so _____ about it.

3. The police were in a _____ about who committed the murder.

4. Jane works for a department store chain and they sent her to Paris to study the latest _____.

5. To help in her _____ chores, Aunt Emma had her own husband tree.

6. The coach told his players that his job was not only to teach, but to _____ them on to do their best.

7. A damp paw can put a _____ on a good time.

8. A worse _____ you would never hope to see; it rained on the Easter parade.

9. Fran told her friends she had the _____ job; working at home on the computer and watching soap operas all day long.

10. Gardeners plant new plants to _____ the old ones.

SONOROUS
(SON uh russ)
producing sound, especially deep
and rich, resonant
Link: **SNORERS**

*"The not-so-SONOROUS SNORERS
of old Santa Fe."*

- ☐ John Barrymore's SONOROUS voice enraptured audiences across the land for decades.

- ☐ The SONORITY of the school choir as they sang Christmas carols in the auditorium was uplifting and delightfully spiritual.

EGALITARIAN

(e gal uh TEAR ee un)

advocating the doctrine of equal rights for all citizens

Link: THE GAL I'M MARRYIN'

"THE GAL I'M MARRYIN' is an EGALITARIAN."

❑ The Communists preached an EGALITARIAN philosophy, but in the end they were the same old fascists the world has known through the ages.

❑ The founders of the Declaration of Independence were no better, they also preached EGALITARIAN principles, yet at the same time they owned slaves.

❑ Martin Luther King was a true EGALITARIAN, he preached for equal rights for all citizens.

DURESS
(DU ress)
hardship, restraint, confinement
Link: CONFESS

*"During interrogation, the suspect was
under DURESS to CONFESS."*

❑ The judge ruled the defendant was under DURESS
when the police got his confession, and therefore
his confession could not be used as evidence.

❑ It is only in recent years that social scientists have
come to understand that many people laboring in
competitive industries are under career DURESS.

VOLITION

(voh LISH un)

an act of choosing, using one's
own will in a conscious choice

Link: **GO FISHIN'**

*"Of his own VOLITION, Bryan would have
preferred to GO FISHIN'."*

- ❑ The biggest question the general had to decide was
  whether the private had cowardly deserted of his
  own VOLITION in the face of the enemy, or as he
  claimed, to rescue a wounded fellow soldier.

- ❑ The dean asked Peter if he was joining a fraternity
  because of peer pressure or his own VOLITION.

ENTREAT
(en TREET)
to ask earnestly; to implore,
plead, beg
Link: **TREAT**

"What is more common than a child ENTREATING a parent for a TREAT of candy or ice cream."

- ☐ Roger said he would ENTREAT Professor Jones to permit us to take the exam early so we could go on the road with the booster club.

- ☐ Our entire family ENTREATED our father to take us on a summer vacation to Europe.

- ☐ The judge listened to the ENTREATIES of the prisoner and decided to give him a suspended sentence because of his family situation.

POTENTATE
(POE tun tate)
a powerful ruler; an important person
Link: **IMPORTANT TATER**

*"A POTENTATE in 'Tater Kingdom' is
an IMPORTANT TATER."*

- ❑ POTENTATES are usually not elected officials, but the descendants of a line of rajahs, sheiks, and emperors, kings and queens.

- ❑ The shah of Iran was an Iranian POTENTATE who lived in the twentieth century.

- ❑ Ever since Sarah was elected president of the junior class, she walks around with her nose in the air, as if she thinks she is a POTENTATE.

DISPARAGE
(dis PEAR ij)
to belittle, say uncomplimentary things;
to put down
Link: **CARRIAGE**

*"The mean step mother DISPARAGED
Cinderella's CARRIAGE."*

- ☐ Pete was told his behavior would DISPARAGE the whole team's efforts.

- ☐ Robert DISPARAGES the accomplishments of his fellow students.

- ☐ Jealousy made Ellen make many DISPARAGING remarks about Rachel's prom dress.

BESET
(bee SET)
to harass; to surround
Link: **BEES SAT**

*"The angry BEES SAT on his face
and BESET the beekeeper."*

❑ We were to have gone to the beach for a sunny vacation, but were BESET with a week of rain and cold weather.

❑ We thought we had the design ironed out, but when three of our aircraft crashed, we knew we were BESET with design problems we had yet to understand.

❑ The losing team was BESET with disappointment.

APPALLING

(uh PAWL ing)

to fill with dismay; causing
horror or consternation

Link: **FALLING**

*"Sue had an APPALLING dream that
she was FALLING."*

❑ It was absolutely APPALLING the way the members of the band taunted the cheerleaders with accusations that their legs looked like twigs.

❑ The travelers received an APPALLING reception at the village hotel; they were given the smallest rooms for the highest prices.

❑ To be APPALLED is to be so horrified as to lose the color or pallor in one's face.

DORMANT
(DOR munt)
asleep or inactive
Link: **DOOR MAT**

"Boys! Boys! Fido may be DORMANT, but he is not a DOOR MAT."

- ❏ Bears hibernate in caves and remain DORMANT throughout the winter.

- ❏ Jim's talent for playing the French horn had been DORMANT for so long he lost his ability to play.

- ❏ The rain fell steadily over the DORMANT village as nightfall approached.

REVIEW #29: Match the word with its definition.

1. sonorous - (snorers)
2. egalitarian - (the gal I'm marryin')
3. duress - (confess)
4. volition - (go fishin')
5. entreat - (treat)
6. potentate - (important tater)
7. disparage - (carriage)
8. beset - (bees sat)
9. appalling - (falling)
10. dormant - (door mat)

a. harass, surround
b. fill with dismay
c. conscious choice
d. resonant sounds
e. asleep, inactive
f. equal rights
g. under restraint
h. important person
i. to put down, belittle
j. to implore, beg

Fill in the blanks with the appropriate word. The word form may need changing.

1. Roger said he would _____ Professor Jones to let us out of class early.

2. Jealousy made Ellen make many _____ remarks abou Sue's prom dress.

3. Sue had an _____ dream that she was falling.

4. The rain fell steadily over the _____ village as nightfall approached.

5. We were to have gone to the beach for a sunny vacation, but were _____ with a week of rain.

6. The shah of Iran was an Iranian _____ who lived in the twentieth century.

7. During interrogation, the suspect was under _____ to confess.

8. John Barrymore was a famous Shakespearean actor with a _____ voice which enraptured audiences.

9. Martin Luther King was a true _____.

10. The dean asked Peter if he was joining a fraternity because of peer pressure or of his own _____.

333

Review Answers

Review #1, page 25
Matching: 1-c 2-d 3-g 4-a 5-f 6-i 7-j 8-h 9-b 10-e
Fill in the Blank: 1-aloof 2-bulwark 3-cacophony
4-chattel 5-incongruous 6-cerebral 7-expunge 8-austere
9-laments 10-connoisseur

Review #2, page 36
Matching: 1-b 2-h 3-c 4-a 5-f 6-i 7-j 8-g 9-e 10-d
Fill in the Blank: 1-migrate 2-asunder 3-roster
4-forbear 5-trenchant 6-procrastinate 7-effaced
8-impede 9-evaded 10-incited

Review #3, page 47
Matching: 1-d 2-e 3-c 4-f 5-j 6-b 7-h 8-a 9-g 10-i
Fill in the Blank: 1-opportune 2-dulcet 3-porcine
4-reminiscent 5-bludgeons 6-beleaguered 7-quixotic
8-arduous 9-milieu 10-histrionic

Review #4, page 58
Matching: 1-f 2-j 3-e 4-h 5-c 6-g 7-i 8-b 9-a 10-d
Fill in the Blank: 1-propulsive 2-askew 3-ambiance
4-enrages 5-coterie 6-cranny 7-ballistics 8-girth
9-lassitude 10-cubism

Review #5, page 69
Matching: 1-d 2-j 3-a 4-i 5-b 6-h 7-e 8-f 9-c 10-g
Fill in the Blank: 1-gossamer 2-harrowing 3-aptitude
4-queue 5-laconic 6-cowered 7-chronic 8-giddy
9-irascible 10-endured

Review #6, page 80
Matching: 1-f 2-h 3-c 4-g 5-e 6-d 7-j 8-i 9-a 10-b
Fill in the Blank: 1-dromedary 2-demonic 3-atrophied
4-harangued 5-noxious 6-grandiloquent 7-caucuses
8-myriad 9-accolade 10-proficient

Review #7, page 91
Matching: 1-j 2-c 3-e 4-b 5-i 6-a 7-h 8-d 9-g 10-f
Fill in the Blank: 1-mustered 2-glutton 3-catapults
4-facilitate 5-mode 6-alienated 7-paranoia 8-beget
9-curtail 10-craven

Review #8, page 102
Matching: 1-i 2-h 3-d 4-f 5-g 6-j 7-b 8-c 9-a 10-e
Fill in the Blank: 1-scrutinize 2-martyr 3-blather
4-doldrums 5-citadels 6-consensus 7-aspired 8-obtuse
9-fjords 10-congenial

Review #9, page 113
Matching: 1-e 2-b 3-a 4-f 5-i 6-c 7-j 8-d 9-g 10-h
Fill in the Blank: 1-curvilinear 2-karma 3-astute
4-draconian 5-artisan 6-resurgent 7-Defamed 8-elapses
9-veered 10-misnomers

Review #10, page 124
Matching: 1-e 2-g 3-a 4-h 5-d 6-j 7-i 8-f 9-b 10-c
Fill in the Blank: 1-guise 2-gird 3-lesions 4-forage
5-fetish 6-dispersed 7-dissolution 8-criterion
9-amenable 10-precariously

Review #11, page 135
Matching: 1-b 2-i 3-a 4-g 5-e 6-c 7-h 8-d 9-j 10-f
Fill in the Blank: 1-denounced 2-fathom 3-divine
4-badgered 5-balm 6-countenance 7-alternative
8-torque 9-docile 10-hovels

Review #12, page 146
Matching: 1-b 2-f 3-h 4-g 5-a 6-e 7-j 8-i 9-c 10-d
Fill in the Blank: 1-elfin 2-claimants 3-wane
4-ensemble 5-tethered 6-aggrandize 7-also-ran
8-chasm 9-erudite 10-fraught

Review #13, page 157
Matching: 1-b 2-a 3-e 4-g 5-d 6-h 7-c 8-i 9-j 10-f
Fill in the Blank: 1-ousted 2-mirages 3-philanthropic
4-entice 5-hoard 6-coups 7-cloister 8-noisome
9-languish 10-misanthropic

Review #14, page 168
Matching: 1-c 2-d 3-j 4-h 5-g 6-b 7-f 8-i 9-e 10-a
Fill in the Blank: 1-deftly 2-antecedent 3-creditors
4-verbatim 5-truncated 6-ubiquitous 7-remorse
8-forsake 9-embodied 10-pillaged

Review #15, page 179
Matching: 1-a 2-b 3-f 4-c 5-i 6-h 7-j 8-d 9-e 10-g
Fill in the Blank: 1-prowess 2-sundry 3-insouciant
4-dearth 5-revered 6-phobia 7-legacy 8-generalize
9-callous 10-somber

Review #16, page 190
Matching: 1-e 2-j 3-a 4-b 5-h 6-i 7-f 8-c 9-d 10-g
Fill in the Blank: 1-gloated 2-ramifications 3-allure
4-commodious 5-paradox 6-penitent 7-edifice 8-pique
9-dispel 10-mused

Review #17, page 201
Matching: 1-d 2-j 3-a 4-h 5-f 6-e 7-i 8-c 9-g 10-b
Fill in the Blank: 1-abhor 2-gazebo 3-euphonious
4-masticate 5-orthodox 6-Archaic 7-callow 8-fawning
9-plight 10-lethargic

Review #18, page 212
Matching: 1-b 2-c 3-f 4-h 5-g 6-d 7-a 8-i 9-j 10-e
Fill in the Blank: 1-cache 2-vertigo 3-oblique 4-quirk
5-comprises 6-bucolic 7-abstruse 8-affidavit
9-dilemma 10-mores

Review #19, page 223
Matching: 1-i 2-j 3-f 4-a 5-h 6-e 7-c 8-g 9-d 10-b
Fill in the Blank: 1-ajar 2-intervene 3-aftermath
4-demur 5-alleviate 6-domain 7-stupefied 8-bleak
9-candor 10-catharsis

Review #20, page 234
Matching: 1-c 2-d 3-a 4-b 5-i 6-g 7-e 8-j 9-h 10-f
Fill in the Blank: 1-melancholy 2-demagogues 3-affinity
4-inveigled 5-Circa 6-lax 7-anterior 8-pied 9-Herbicide
10-bizarre

Review #21, page 245
Matching: 1-c 2-a 3-b 4-i 5-j 6-f 7-h 8-d 9-g 10-e
Fill in the Blank: 1-abuts 2-wither 3-perverse 4-petulant
5-embellish 6-assuage 7-serpentine 8-segregated
9-castigated 10-wrested

Review #22, page 256
Matching: 1-d 2-c 3-e 4-a 5-g 6-f 7-j 8-b 9-h 10-i
Fill in the Blank: 1-marshaled 2-grandiose 3-desiccate
4-relinquish 5-enraptured 6-fortuitous 7-unbridled
8-surfeit 9-photogenic 10-guile

Review #23, page 267
Matching: 1-h 2-c 3-b 4-a 5-g 6-d 7-f 8-e 9-j 10-i
Fill in the Blank: 1-cajole 2-emulate 3-atypical
4-bereaving 5-loiter 6-tyro 7-abyss 8-adjunct 9-yore
10-idiosyncrasy

Review #24, page 278
Matching: 1-b 2-c 3-e 4-i 5-d 6-h 7-g 8-j 9-a 10-f
Fill in the Blank: 1-certify 2-lexicon 3-lieu 4-amplified
5-permeated 6-partitions 7-maimed 8-evoke 9-deduce
10-menagerie

Review #25, page 289
Matching: 1-d 2-g 3-a 4-c 5-b 6-j 7-i 8-e 9-h 10-f
Fill in the Blank: 1-infamies 2-entomology 3-capacious
4-fickle 5-fleeced 6-Nepotism 7-jousted 8-parried
9-periphery 10-ostracized

Review #26, page 300
Matching: 1-h 2-j 3-a 4-i 5-e 6-b 7-d 8-g 9-f 10-c
Fill in the Blank: 1-rudimentary 2-marauding 3-umbrage
4-abomination 5-riveted 6-emit 7-engulfed 8-abridged
9-entombed 10-festered

Review #27, page 311
Matching: 1-g 2-j 3-h 4-c 5-e 6-b 7-i 8-a 9-f 10-d
Fill in the Blank: 1-feigned 2-laudable 3-exhume
4-debased 5-spurn 6-Dauntless 7-altercation 8-gamins
9-chided 10-decree

Review #28, page 322
Matching: 1-d 2-j 3-a 4-e 5-f 6-h 7-i 8-g 9-c 10-b
Fill in the Blank: 1-scapegoat 2-truculent 3-quandary
4-couture 5-husbandry 6-spur 7-damper 8-debacle
9-optimum 10-supplant

Review #29, page 333
Matching: 1-d 2-f 3-g 4-c 5-j 6-h 7-i 8-a 9-b 10-e
Fill in the Blank: 1-entreat 2-disparaging 3-appalling
4-dormant 5-beset 6-potentate 7-duress 8-sonorous
9-egalitarian 10-volition

Index

Ordering Information

**Vocabulary Cartoons,
Elementary Edition**
3rd – 6th Grade
ISBN: 0965242277

**Vocabulary Cartoons,
SAT Word Power**
7th – 12th Grade
ISBN: 0965242285

**Vocabulary Cartoons,
SAT Word Power II**
7th – 12th Grade
ISBN: 0965242269

Attention Schools:
Quantity discounts are available.
Blackline Masters and Overhead
Transparencies are also available.
For more information and a free brochure call:
1 –800-741-1295

New Monic Books, Inc.
314-C Tamiami Trail
Punta Gorda, Florida 33950
(941) 575-6463 fax
www.vocabularycartoons.com